Editorial

T0026820

Donne is not alone when he writes, in 'The Autumnal',

> I hate extremes, yet I had rather stay
> With tombs than cradles, to wear out a day.

Writers generally feel comfortable in a necropolis. At least they did when I was younger. There is a sense of permanency if not of presence among the tombs and the eroding words they speak. Death has undone so many, Dante remarks. In Père Lachaise, the Isola de San Michele, Hampstead or Bunhill Fields, there is no lack of visitors (historians, critics, Methodists, modernists, tourists, Marxists), hungry for inscriptions, for that intense sense of presence that absence sometimes brings. They deposit a daisy or a rose in Bunyan's or Baudelaire's vicinity, picking simples. Keats's cancelled line, 'the feel of not to feel it', comes to mind. If you 'Go forward beyond the tombs' – one of Flaubert's favourite tags from Goethe – you end up in the modern town or city that hems the cemetery in on all sides, or in the lagoon.

Flaubert has a horror of endings. In 1866 he wrote to George Sand, 'Each one of us carries within himself his necropolis.' Also to Sand, 'I am gorged with coffins like an old graveyard!' But to go beyond the tombs entails going through the graveyard in the first place, not skirting round it. To come to terms with the worn paths, the dead flowers, the chipped inscriptions. We might read *Salambô*, gorgeous, tedious, exhaustively researched, as a necropolis, or the hilarious graveyard of illusions that is *Bouvard et Pécuchet*... these necessary preparations, exercises in *self*-effacement, for the tremendous impersonal labour that went into inventing the present tenses of *Madame Bovary* and *L'Éducation sentimental*.

The coffins Flaubert is gorged with contain played-out formal and thematic commonplaces, familiar clichés which he has incorporated into his practice, which first enable and then restrain him. Like habits he has to break. 'Go forward beyond the tombs.' Irony is a walking stick.

In the second chapter of *Bouvard et Pécuchet*, the two eccentric friends in their attempt to connect learning and life conduct their collaborative 'Experiments in Agriculture'. They design their garden. 'Pécuchet made several diagrams, while using his mathematical case. Bouvard gave him advice. They arrived at no satisfactory result.' Having failed to be original, they resort to the pattern books. By fortune, good or bad, they find in their inexhaustible library Boitard's *L'Architecte des Jardins*. 'The author divides [gardens] into a great number of styles,' including 'the melancholy and romantic style, which is distinguished by immortelles, ruins, tombs'; the terrible style with cliffs, blasted trees, ruins; the 'exotic style', with Peruvian torch-thistles, 'to arouse memories in a colonist or a traveller'; the grave style with a temple dedicated to philosophy; the 'majestic style' with obelisks, triumphal arches; the 'mysterious style', mossy and be-grottoed; the 'dreamy style' with a lake and other unexpected features. 'Before this horizon of marvels, Bouvard and Pécuchet experienced a kind of bedazzlement.' We note how each of the styles pertains to a fashion of cemetery furniture, from the classical to the gothic.

They invest in a faux-Etruscan tomb, sacrificing the asparagus patch to situate it at the heart of things. 'Four little pine trees at the corners flanked the monument, which was to be surmounted by an urn and enriched by an inscription.' Alas, 'In the twilight it looked dreadful. The rockery, like a mountain, covered the entire grass plot; the tomb formed a cube in the midst of spinaches, the Venetian bridge a circumflex over the kidney-beans, and the summer-house beyond a big black spot, for they had burned its straw roof to make it more poetic.' Bouvard and Pécuchet are enchanted to witness 'their guests' astonishment'. Errors of judgement are likened to misplaced punctuation marks, failures of style.

Flaubert knew what he was doing. To George Sand he said: 'one should not… put one's personality into the picture. I think that great art is scientific and impersonal. One should, by an effort of mind, put oneself into one's characters and not create them after oneself. That is the method at least…' Then he exclaims, 'How vain are all the poetic theories and criticisms! – and the nerve of the gentlemen who compose them sickens me.'

Writers nowadays – the kind who distrust tombs and cradles -- espouse theories of another kind, that precede the kind of dedicated reading that led to 'The Autumnal', *Les fleurs du mal* or *Personae* and may even strive to invalidate them on the grounds of contemporary issues strictly irrelevant to their existence (one daren't say to their composition, because if one returns the finished work to its process one reintroduces what the writer spent great efforts to expel, and excuses the theorist to read the life rather than the work).

Words have intentions and then 'second intentions'. Some writers compose with the intention and second intention in mind at the same time, producing an explicit and an inferred text. In great works of poetry, fewer of prose, the second intention is just about sufficient: in passages of Christopher Smart, or Samuel Taylor Coleridge, or Gertrude Stein, Marianne Moore or Wallace Stevens; even, perhaps, of Eliot, in the Sweeney poems and 'Prufrock', maybe in 'The Waste Land'. We might say second intention is elevated above first: how the poem says not what the poem says; or *how* the poem says is what the poem says. This is not the case with the poetry of some of our voluble necropolis-averse contemporaries who nourish their art on an imagined future rich in relevance and leave the realised past ('a circumflex over the kidney beans') well buried. They don't *leave it behind*; they have not gone that way.

Letters to the Editor

Anthony Rudolf writes: I was pleased to read Colin Still's generous, perceptive and instructive account of Michael Horovitz in *PNR* 261. One regret: there was no mention of the poet Inge Else Laird, a key figure in his life for quite a few years. She is well remembered by those who knew and loved her. Michael in an obituary note in the *Guardian* in 2011 evoked 'the near ego-less purity of her aspira-

tions and achievements'.

Peter Popham writes: Interesting editorial in no 261, just arrived. You seem on the verge of saying something. Then in the gnomic final paragraph you funk it. I think you owe Chimene and Co a more robust conclusion.

News & Notes

Luis Alberto de Cuenca · *El Pais* on 21 October reported that Luis Alberto de Cuenca received a phone call telling him he had won the 2021 García Lorca Prize for poetry in honour of the full trajectory of his work (he is now seventy years old). The poet was amused, and of course pleased, to join the company of such outstanding writers as José Emilio Pacheco, Francisco Brines and Ida Vitale who got there before him. His latest book, a collection of a hundred new poems, *Después del paraíso* (*After Paradise*) was recently published by Visor. The book was composed against the grain during the pandemic: silent and dry, as he describes himself, he was suddenly visited by four unexpected lines and they became the engine of the book. He found the book, he said, 'useful' to his survival. He describes himself as having been a straight-forward, plain poet who is becoming darker and more difficult as he progresses. He and Pere Gimferrer are the first poets of the 1990s to receive the prize which is intended to honour a poet from any Spanish-speaking country.

Pablo Neruda · To mark the fiftieth anniversary of his being awarded the Nobel Prize for Literature, *La Terracera* reported, the publisher Seix Barral would publish on 21 October a boxed five-volume set (adding up to 3,692 pages) of the poetry of Pablo Neruda. All forty of his books are included. The volumes have been available singly but this monumental gathering of his legacy feels and looks definitive. The fourth volume

contains a selection of all the scattered works and uncollected material so far discovered, with dedicatory poems to fellow Chilean and Latin American writers and occasional poems dedicated to Puerto Rico and Cuba.

Harvard · The *Taiwan Times* on 12 October reported that Harvard University had decided to transfer its Mandarin Chinese summer program from Beijing to National Taiwan University in Taipei in summer 2022. The programme director recorded 'a perceived lack of friendliness' from Beijing Language and Culture University, according to the Harvard *Crimson*. Problems started when access to dormitories and classrooms became problematic. 'Given the conditions they provided, we really couldn't run the program with the quality that we are hoping to deliver to our students.' Possibly the change, she suggested, was due to the shifting sense Beijing has of American institutions. The American government's National Security Education Program had also moved its Mandarin language training to Taiwan, to the Chinese Overseas Flagship in Taiwan in 2019. Many of Harvard's China programmes are staying in China.

Jean 'Binta' Breeze · *SuAndi writes:* Looking back, it was pretty reckless of me to take on the role of co-host with Lemn Sissay the same night as my very first performance as a poet. I wasn't even calling myself a poet then. But I did. The evening consisted of Cultureword Identity Writers and the cream of Black writers; Grace Nichols, John Agard and Jean Binta Breeze. I was to introduce Breeze so I approached her to ask how she wanted to be presented, 'By my name,' she fired back at me. Breeze was fierce, a trait that I have heard to describe myself over the years. But Breeze's fierce-ness was that of a lioness: she not only roared, she could bite.

I was fortunate to share many other performances with her and at almost all of them she would refuse to perform my favourite piece about the woman with the radio in her head but then at the end she would perform it, giving me a wide grin.

Looking back at her career it is understandable that she carried an inner strength born out of the fact that she was regarded as the first lady of Dub.

I never heard her speak of her childhood. Born 1956, she was raised in Hanover Parish, Jamaica, by her grandparents who were 'peasant farmers' so I don't imagine there was money aplenty. But someone must have spotted her talent and drive as she went on to study at the Jamaican School of

Drama. It is not surprising that she became recognised as a teacher, theatre director, actor and choreographer. Jean often sang during her performances, but for my ears she was never really a singer.

It was not until the seventies that she started to write poetry and rock the world of DUB which until then was a male bastion. Mutabaruka immediately recognised her talent and was the first to record her.

Thanks to Francia Messado for sending me the press link late on the night her death was announced. Instinctively I reached out to LKJ as I know Linton and she were close. I'm not going to say I shared the same level of friendship, but over the years Breeze and I shared a lot of time and gigs.

When she was directed by Yvonne Brewster for Talawa Theatre's production of Shange's play, I travelled to London in support. Jean was in a grumpy mood accepting a drink from my fella who had been blown away by the show, but refusing to speak to the Scottish man.

In Manchester she often stayed at mine, one time with her daughter. Breeze had been on the brandy so when I heard her daughter tell her there was a black cake box under the bed, I was thankful that she told the child to go asleep. A little later, on hearing Breeze in slumber, I crept into the bedroom to remove the box to the safety of my own cupboard. (I did tell Breeze sometime later that I had removed the cake box because it contains my father's ashes and she thumped me hard. I mean really hard.)

Time passed before I spent an afternoon in a bar with her and Agard at some university event where we were reading. I wanted to talk about her wonderful short stories, I loved the one about cricket and the patent leather shoes of the little girl, but she was reminiscing with John, and I sat and listened. Later she benefited from the professional support and care of Melanie Abrahams (Renaissance One). I went to the Leicester University event lead by Corrine Fowler (a mentor to me and who later became my friend). She had nominated Breeze and later me as

Writing Fellows. And that was the last time I saw her.

Brendan Kennelly · The Irish poet Brendan Kennelly has died, at the age of eighty-five. He had returned to his native North Kerry some years ago, the place he had left, as a scholarship winner, for Trinity College Dublin. An outsider at Trinity as a student, he nonetheless returned there after graduate study at Leeds, initially as a junior lecturer, becoming Professor of Modern Literature, a role he occupied from 1973 to his retirement in 2005. He was an inspirational teacher, and as editor of *Icarus*, would publish and befriend younger gifted student poets, including Eavan Boland and Michael Longley. Longley would later edit, with Terence Brown, *The Essential Brendan Kennelly* (Bloodaxe, 2011), and wrote of this work, "It remains for me one of the best things I've ever done. I loved and revered the man and his words."

Kennelly was easily the most famous poet in Ireland during the 1980s, a regular on radio and tv chat shows and a non-driver who was the voiceover star of Toyota radio ads. He had by then shifted away from crisp and often agonizing lyric poems to long poems in which he adopted personae, 'epic ballads' as his friend Gabriel Fitzmaurice called them, which took on the voices of scapegoats, *Cromwell* and *The Book of Judas*, whose admirers included, among others, the singer Bono, who quoted *The Book of Judas* when addressing a US university audience: 'If you want to serve the age, betray it.'

Máire Mhac tSaoi · Máire Mhac an tSaoi, who has died aged ninety-nine, named her autobiography *The Same Age as the State*. Her Belfast-born father, Seán McEntee, had fought in the GPO in 1916 and would serve as Fianna Fáil minister for finance, and as Tánaiste, while her mother, Margaret Browne, was also active in the Rising.

Mhac an tSaoi went to school Dún Chaoin, in the Kerry Gaeltacht, and took a degree in Celtic Studies and Modern Languages, which led

to her publishing research on Irish Arthurian Romances. After training as a barrister, she joined the civil service. Her first collection, *Margadh na Saoire*, appeared in 1956 and soon after her highly critical review of Sean Seán Ó Ríordáin's *Eireaball Spideoige*, which established the polarities of modern Irish-language poetry, with her work's interest in continuities in the tradition seen as rejecting some of the modernizing bareness of Ó Ríordáin's work.

After marrying politician and journalist Conor Cruise O'Brien, she lived for a time in Ghana with him, where they adopted two children, before returning to Dublin. Never shy of controversy, she was arrested for anti-war protests, and would resign her position in Ireland's assembly of artists Aosdána over her criticism of a peer's anti-Semitism. She continued writing, not just poetry but also fiction and a translation into Irish of Rilke, and was a notable encourager of younger women poets. In 2011, poet and critic Louis de Paor edited a landmark selection of her work *The Miraculous Parish / An Paróiste Míorúilteach* (O'Brien Press)

Grey Gowrie · *Stanley Moss writes*, in a draft of his elegy to the poet Grey, Lord Gowrie, a *PN Review* contributor and friend:

Grey, Lord of two hearts,
your heart has become a
    shoreless ocean.
On the *Third Day* of creation,
dry land, plants, trees, and ocean,
you judged yourself, no
    absolution.
You are now apart
from those who love you,
manners, love, poetry, body, soul
    were you.
You know 'happiness blooms in
    small corners.'
Calliope is among your mourners.
Now you are among the most
    ordinary
dead and the most extraordinary
with Callimachus,
the least superfluous.

His full name was Alexander Patrick Greysteil Hore-Ruthven, Lord

Gowrie. He was eighty-one at the time of his death. As well as being a political figure (quondam chancellor of the Duchy of Lancaster) he left politics because the ministerial salary could not support his lifestyle. He was most visible as Minister for the Arts for two years under Mrs Thatcher. He became European chair of Sotheby's and then chair of the Arts Council. His connections with poetry developed at Oxford and took a curious turn when at Buffalo University in upstate New York he encountered the Black Mountain poets and then, at Harvard, he assisted Robert Lowell, establishing a durable friendship. In 1969 he was back in the UK, teaching at UCL and taking the Conservative whip in the House of Lords (he had assumed the title aty the age of fifteen).

His first collection of poems was published in 1972, *A Postcard from Don Giovanni*. Though his output was sporadic, he built up a significant body of work. When *Third Day: New and Selected Poems* was published in 2008, Derek Mahon wrote in the *Irish Times*, 'Grey Gowrie's great *Third Day: New and Selected Poems* – a fine, stoical portrait of the age – fulfils all expectations'. It was a distillation of his life's work, from 1958 onward. The book centred on the sequence 'The Domino Hymn: Poems from Harefield', published in 2005. It builds from his year spent at Harefield when, on the threshold of death, he was given a heart transplant. His most recent full collection, *The Italian Visitor* (2013), included a memoir of Robert Lowell.

A Rainbow for Callie Gardner (1990–2021) · *Maria Stedmere writes:* I was about to get on a train when I first received news that Callie Gardner had passed suddenly on the 8 July. A prolific poet, critic and editor of the magazine and micro-press *Zarf* (2015-2020), Callie was a devoted supporter of many campaigns for political and social justice, to community organising and creating safe and nurturing spaces for marginalised writers. Their presence touched so many people: from queer folks all over the world who read their work, to the lucky ones who knew Callie as a tutor, editor or publisher, to the many friends and comrades they made through poetry and activist spaces such as the Small Trans Library. After earning a PhD from Cardiff University, Callie forged a life outside of the academy, running workshops at Glasgow's queer bookshop Category Is, contributing to numerous reading groups and offering writing experiments and striking commentaries on contemporary poems through their blogs, *misleadingly like lace* and *the second moon letters*.

Callie was, to quote a close friend Gloria Dawson, 'like an encyclopaedia that loves you back': they had exquisitely detailed and lively knowledge on everything from space physics to emoji lore and the wallabies of Loch Lomond, and would offer it in enthusiastic bubbles of anecdote and dialogue. I cherished their secret streak of humour and wit – what the poet Dom Hale once admired as Callie's unabashed love of the pun – and the generosity, nuance and care in everything they did. The education and poetics Callie championed were horizontal, sprawling, collaborative, beyond institutions:

a kind of meadowing in common, available for everyone willing, (bio) diverse with mutual space to grow.

In all their attention to the (un) doings of language, its gatherings and play (especially in their work as a scholar of Roland Barthes), its social potential and material conditions, I think of Callie as a builder of ongoing worlds. Their book, *naturally it is not: a poem in four letters* (the87press, 2018) is an epistolary venture in what it means to queer, to compost, to be against 'nature' and the closed readings of what Veronica Forrest-Thomson calls 'bad Naturalisation'. It's a processual, multifarious work between seasons, scenarios, places, the portable work of address and citation which is a moving present: 'going through time in this way i wish you were here'.

Back in 2018, in the final issue of a magazine I used to edit, *Gilded Dirt*, we published their poem 'where it was you meant to travel', which ends: 'what a glow / emerges from the place where i might otherwise have been!' It always struck me that Callie is and was a poet of transit and transmutation, and I find proof as I write this, on the train heading north and homewards to Glasgow: a rainbow appears and is gone, but still a gift to be proffered in *naturally it is not* – 'rainbows hide; wish mine were yours'. As they describe in their *Granta* essay 'Terminology', Callie's 'unscientific utopia' is a fantasy sleeper train called 'Iris', named 'after the Roman goddess of the rainbow': a place 'on the move' where "everything is gay and nothing hurts". Amidst lived precarity, it's one abundance among many that Callie gave us, of wish and demand, what a glow.

Reports

On Not Listening Quietly

VAHNI CAPILDEO

'Terrific, terrific, terrific,' the tall lady with perfectly maintained blonde hair and a far from new, exquisitely tailored navy blazer roared. She was sitting in front of me at one of those curious events that gather poets and non-poets, sometimes the royal, or the very rich. Beginning as quiet as a wax museum figure, upright and polite, she had proceeded to liven up to real interest in the poetry being performed. You could see the rigid lines of her silhouette soften. Her breathing changed with her listening. She subsided a little in her seat. She paused. She seemed unsure how to show appreciation. Then she fell back on her accustomed vocabulary. 'Terrific.'

Up to that point, less enthralled by the poetry, I had entertained myself by admiring the stitching on her clothes. Too much a craftsperson, I had dropped attention from the thin texts being offered up to the mixed public and turned to the art visible in delicate expensive textiles, the concept and structure brought into being by unknown persons' handiwork. She, however, was feeling a thrill, like someone at a sports match. 'Marvellous, marvellous, marvellous!' She cried out as if we were at Wimbledon. She cried out as if the words released by the poet deserved a return of some kind, from the heart. And why not?

People talk about missing the live element from performance, during the pandemic, when events were relocated online or did not happen at all. Paradoxically, the live element was what I used to miss from in-person performances. Why was it that audiences seemed to coffin and confine themselves to the narrowest possible range of response, at least off the slam circuit? I refuse the easy answers, 'respect' and 'culture', as too sad, too deathly; as if respect had to take the form of mute submission, and as if culture were synonymous with blank-ing out the body. Have you been among people who shout 'Preach!' 'Word!' or 'You lie!'? How often have you wanted to whoop, or stamp? Would you do this in contexts where poetry is not a million miles from revolution or parlour? What about in contexts where you want to bring the revolution or take the breeze in a parlour? What are the many little ways that a 'reading' can progress more like an encounter, less like a delivery? During Zoom sessions I enjoy seeing participants feel free to switch off their cameras. It encourages me to see absurd emojis redden and yellow the screen. Cartoon hearts float, signalling an audience full of bounce. Out of sight, they have freedom of movement.

Upright and polite, in-person audiences sit quiet as if being inoculated with poetry, not galvanized; as if being spoon-fed poetry, not plunging wilfully into a cold stream, gasping and drinking. What is the internal cost, or effect, of this? Is it a positive self-stilling, while the meditative interior comes alive? Is it self-censorship, a refusal to be moved, all present and correct? There was that violinist in Florence who threw his lion-head back and brought it forward to growl at his violin. He stamped back and forth, right to the edge of the stage. These sounds would have been edited out in a recording studio. They were not part of his 'act'. The music, his idea of it, was picking him up and flinging him about. His connexion with his instrument was a full-body process. He breathed with his arm movements, as much an athlete as any unnamed pearl diver or sponsored Olympic swimmer. The sounds he made as a musician would not have been possible without the sounds he emitted as an embodied being, making music. Why don't poetry lovers make sounds and movements back?

Perhaps, in getting away from the nonsense praise of verse as 'full-blooded', 'muscular' and 'masculine', or the nonsense idea that people's physical lung capacity determines the reach of their poetic line, we are so much in flight from toxic celebrations of power that we forget that messy, rowdy, leaping joy does not have to indicate a lapse in care. On the other hand, perhaps practising contained forms of listening is paradoxically a way of opening oneself to extreme states of in-betweenness and fragility, words beyond body and silence beyond words; allowing oneself to be carried-towards or carried-with, rather than carried away. Perhaps quiet listening is highly political, not in the sense I earlier suspected, not a symptom of being schooled in deference, but in the sense of strengthening attention to what is slow and gradual *as well as* immediate, vulnerable *as well as* impulsive or superb. Shyness is not the same as reticence, which is not the same as suppression.

In the last stages of the winter lockdown spanning 2020 to 2021, the quiet fishing village where I live ceased to be quiet in the nights, only for short intervals, but repeatedly. As winter peaked, in February, and as midnight after midnight approached, people ran howling down the streets. It is a distinct way of producing the voice; full-bodied, from the ground up, full-breathed abdomen, lungs pumping with red sound. I had heard something like it coming over the mountains ahead of storms. I had heard something like it on pre-pandemic nights, when the clock slid over and groups moved from the pubs that had closed to the clubs that stayed open. I had not previously heard howling for its own sake. Men were turning into wolves or letting out the wolf in them. To what does a wolf respond?

In the relative local ease of summer 2021, walking through a port, I heard drumming and shouting from a junction. I looked for the drummers, imagining a festival. There was a group of men beating their chests. Beating their own chests ritually, they produced the rhythmic sound of great drums. No women accompanied them in any way. Instead of a festival of dancing, instead of channelling gods, shouting rather than singing, big men stood in a cluster. A smaller man quietly leafleted for some cause. I was tempted to talk to the leafleter, if only to add mixed voices in conversational exchange to the fringe of the rousing, obliterating soundscape. I did not stop. It struck me that the sound of their insides and the sound of their outsides had become one, and that sound was bouncing off the surrounding buildings. Anyone walking past listening to other music or talking to another person would become absorbed into that body of sound temporarily as they passed. Perhaps the well-behaved poetry audiences are wary of the continuous production of self-sound; then again, that might be a case for responding to the poets...

Dying and living with de la Mare

SUBHA MUKHERJI

On the last night of the blighted year just past, I suddenly woke up because I thought I heard a noise at the door: knock or whistle. I could not tell what hour it was. I stumbled downstairs to check my garden door and then my front door. Had I dreamt it? The whistle was a wild wind. The knock – it was someone, or something, I was sure, though my eyes just met darkness. But, like Bottom, and any audience in Shakespeare's theatre, I was hearing sights (and perhaps seeing sounds too). In fact I thought I knew, for a minute, that it was Ma – my mother, who had died on Christmas day in Kolkata, while I was stuck here in cold and dark Cambridge, desperately and ceaselessly trying to get home to India through successive flight cancellations and Covid chaos. I was desperate because place seemed to matter. But perhaps it doesn't to the dead. And it must not, to the living, when they want to hear-see the dead, and hear-say with them, against distance and spatial reality – a heresy best expressed not in prose but in poetic form, perhaps even in rhyme:

Someone came knocking
At my wee small door;
Someone came knocking,
I'm sure – sure – sure...

The theatrical analogy is pertinent. Ma was inherently dramatic: she took part in amateur theatricals all her life, wherever she found herself – from her crowded household with eight siblings as she was growing up, to stageplays at social clubs later in life. She also read and loved poetry in her youth and remembered it, fitfully, in age. And she was fascinated by ghost stories: the only person in our house who knew and loved de la Mare's stories as well as his poems. Her theatricality and her pleasure in the fiction of phantoms came together in impish pranks she played on people – she got into terrible trouble once when she scared her newish sister-in-law by springing on her from behind a cupboard dressed like a goblin in the night, her face obscured with pale gauze.

However, my first exposure to de la Mare did not come through Ma. When I was growing up in the Kolkata of the 70s, Dada (my grandfather), a man of letters and a polymath, used to hold a morning soirée every Sunday. Four to six of his friends would gather, converse, read together, recite poems from memory – usually Sanskrit epics or Bengali poetry – and discuss literature and politics. They always overstayed their welcome. By lunch-time, my mother and grandmother would start fretting and giving out signs: then the men would grudgingly disperse and lunch would be served. I was the go-between – flitting from kitchen and domestic interior to drawing room. Unofficially a listener, officially I was a page-finder! I had nick-names for all the 'grandads' or 'dadus': 'cigarette-dadu' (chain-smoking grandad), 'golpo-dadu' (story-grandad), and so on. One of them, Pramathanath Bishi, author and parliamentarian, was 'Contents-grandad' ('suchipatra-dadu'): he would call me every time they needed to look up a poem or a passage that they half-remembered. It was at one of these gatherings that Dada recited a de la Mare poem – I found the page but it wasn't needed.

From then, I was hooked: Dada and I would often recite his poems together or read them out aloud from Palgrave's Golden Treasury or its ilk. In the Kolkata of my childhood there was no snobbery against poetic anthologies, let alone any post-modern embarrassment about rhyme. It being a self-delightingly oral culture, rhythm and rhyme were among the matter of everyday exchange.

Nor did this culture have any sense of alienation from haunting – the otherworldly and its imaginative possibilities which, to me, was the substance of de la Mare's poetry. No wonder he was popular. I, and many others, knew his poems by heart.

But last autumn, when I was at home for nine weeks with Ma as she was battling multiple illnesses and slowly slipping away, I recalled a de la Mare poem imperfectly. Living in the UK for thirty odd years had made me lame in memory and an expert in web-recall! But I had been re-membering old favourite poems (and songs) with Ma in her sick-room whenever she was responsive; the wifi was often non-responsive, so our memories were at work. A lot of Tagore, some nursery rhymes – sweet and vicious in equal degrees – and, one day, de la Mare. I recited 'The Listeners' to her, an anthology favourite. And then 'Autumn (November)', which we had both always found haunting: 'There is wind where the rose was...'. On the second stanza, I stumbled:

Nought warm where your hand was,
Nought gold where your hair was...

I looked at Ma. Largely paralysed and speechless at this point, unable to manage any complete sentence, she looked up and clearly reeled off the next few lines (though she forgot the 'but'):

[But] phantom, forlorn,
Beneath the thorn,
Your ghost where your face was.

I had joined in time for the final line of the verse – she had jogged my memory and it all came flooding back in. It was a moment, among others, when I recognised that poetic form was the medium of the dying; not connected or sequential prose. The number of times Ma filled in my gaps was countless, during that brief phase of livelier-than-life-ness; sometimes articulately, sometimes mouthing the words, but unmistakeably. Surprised by joy every time, I went on to yet more poems and songs, the years fell away, and the old Ma broke through. The young, and then still young, woman who was my friend once, voracious and wildly imaginative, and with whom I shared stories, poems, songs and tales of my teenage romance. This time, verses with a pronounced beat – think of the ballad-rhyme of 'The Listeners' – were the ones she remembered most vividly, almost in an extra-cognitive, bodily sense. Perhaps rhythm and rhyme flow in where the heart's beats have slowed, perhaps these poems were the pulse she was 'wanting' – in both senses; quickening her breath even as it felt its own end, its reach. Little did we know then that in the end Covid would take her breath away.

But the pathway between lacking breath and longing for it was a continuum for her. De la Mare's poetry, thus, was a medium she inhabited easily, and thought with. For his work defies the absolute otherness of the dead while it feels in its heart, like his Traveller, death's 'strangeness'. As I watch her being reconstructed after death as a radical non-conformist – we the living often need to rewrite our dead – I remember, bemused, how much she resonated with the imaginative life of rituals and how fun she found them; how much she liked little domestic 'pujas' or worship-fests; how intimately she spoke to her cabinetful of little idols in the assurance that they surely understood that she had had too many concerts and parties in a given fortnight to have done her prayers but of course she was as devoted as ever; and how she spoke of the dead as though they were just across a window, listening, listened to, and ready to be invited in for tea and samosas. The Ma I want to hold on to was this hilariously composite and poignantly paradoxical creature who revelled in secular pleasures as easily as she communed with what might lie beyond; the woman who, only a year ago, suggested to my friend Aveek that they get together to 'call Tapan-da down' (a beloved uncle, the late Tapan Raychaudhuri, an eminent historian with whom she had a deeply fond and sweetly jokey relationship) so that they could have the chat of their lives, or 'narak-guljar': a Bengali phrase for turning-hell-into-paradise with 'adda' – vibrant chatter and carousing. When Aveek suggested she should go ahead with her planchette (séance) till he found a window, she quickly replied: 'I don't want all the wrong spirits flocking in like creepie-crawlies! I need you here, so that I'm not spooked out and we can settle down with cups of tea because Tapan-da is a raconteur'. And then she giggled. The tense she used for these imagined addas was the present. She was too intuitive a liver-of-life to articulate or theorise this, but these fantasies of return were a continual negotiation of death, and what we want to do with it in our imaginative lives. It was, for her, 'what heart heard of, ghost guessed' (Hopkins), like the lines of de la Mare which came back to her so effortlessly through the back-door when she could barely think 'straight' – poetry's own haunting, defying the logic of sequent time. De la Mare would have understood her, and the culture out of which that peculiarly amphibian sensibility took shape. She, and it, understood him.

And as for the play and mischief that reading de la Mare through Ma, and speaking to her through him, wove into his hushed, melancholy yearning: I'd like to think he wouldn't mind too much. He might even smile, if he was listening, at the puckish wink I got from Ma – she could not speak that day – when on a November night, before returning to the UK, I told her that since she enjoyed believing in ghosts, if she became one, she should come and visit me – we would have fun. 'Every wink of an eye some new grace [was] born' – to misquote *The Winter's Tale*, but also to relive it.

Another night. I'm still here as I have failed to travel, and have settled into a kind of hospitality across the threshold. I'm reading 'The Song of Shadows':

Ghosts linger in the darkening air,
Hearken at the open door;
Music hath called them, dreaming,

Home once more.

Between loving and losing, here and there, known and unknowable, the rain taps and the wind knocks at the garden door. I listen, but I don't open – I need not; perhaps I need not to. A de la Mare threshold across which Ma, too, may one day choose to enter; or where she may at least hover and 'whisper awhile'. Unwonted desire, offspring of whimsical grief, might tip dream over into encounter. Ghost and face might shimmer into one another and merge. Through 'a history of come and gone', we would both have kept our word, and come home.

'The Little Trobairitz' (a School Play)

SARAH WHITE

Scene: window of a castle in Die, department of Drôme,

Provence
Time: early thirteenth century
The very young Countess of Día looks out the castle window and converses with her Uncle.

COUNTESS   Uncle, I'm beautiful, of good mind and lineage. I should marry a powerful lord, shouldn't I?
UNCLE   I'm working on it, Niece – we're deep in negotiations.
COUNTESS   With whom, Uncle and Guardian?
UNCLE   Lord Guilhem de Poitou.
COUNTESS   Guilhem the troubadour? Wonderful! *She begins to sing:*
   Farai un vers de dreit rien ...
   I'll make a song from absolutely nothing
   ... composed while sleeping
   and on horseback...
UNCLE   That Guilhem died years ago, my dear. The Guilhem I'm talking to is his grandson. Other possibilities are his great-grandson, Guilhem, and his great-nephews, Guilhem and Guilhem. If they don't work out, there's a distant cousin also named...
COUNTESS   I see that Guilhem de Poitou is bound to be my husband. I think I'll call him 'Willy Nilly.' I wonder if I'll love him. I would like to be in love when I'm married.
UNCLE   You will be, my dear, but not with Guilhem. You'll love another knight – Lord Raimbaut d'Aurenga – whom you'll meet at your wedding feast:
COUNTESS   Raimbaut, the troubadour? *(sings)*
   Ara resplan la flor inversa...
   Now the inverted flower blooms
   On rocky ledge, on hilly slope.
   What flower? Snow, ice, frozen
   Rains that burn, torment, and slice...
UNCLE   Enough! That Raimbaut's too old. Your *amic* will be a young relation of his – fine horseman, I hear – not a bit musical.
COUNTESS   But I am so musical! I'll become a troubadour and compose many good songs about him! *(sings)*
   Sapchatz gran talan n'auria
   que.us tengues en luoc del marit...
   Be sure I'd have a strong desire
   to have you in my husband's place.
UNCLE   Ho! I see Lord Guillem will be marrying a vixen! But you can't become a troubadour, Niece. You have to be a *trobairitz.*
COUNTESS   Can a *trobairitz* strap on a lute, ride to other castles, and sing?
UNCLE   Certainly not! You can't trot around entertaining at feasts like a common *jongleur.* Not even a troubadour does that if he's well born.

COUNTESS   But two great troubadours – Arnaut Daniel and Gaucelm Faidit (the fat one) – were here just last month entertaining.

UNCLE   That's because they needed the money. You will have enough money.

COUNTESS   *(weeps)*

UNCLE   *Oy* Niece. Having money is nothing to weep about!

COUNTESS   It is if I can't go to courts and feasts.

UNCLE   You can go, but you'll arrange for your songs to be performed by a jongleur. That's necessary in order to outwit the gossips.

COUNTESS   Then how will people know the songs are mine? How will Raimbaut know they're for him?

UNCLE   You can drop hints.

COUNTESS   And he'll understand them? What if only the gossips understand them, and Raimbaut isn't even there?

UNCLE   Then you'll arrange for a messenger to carry them to his estate and sing them.

COUNTESS   How lovely for him! And will he reward me with the devotion I deserve?

UNCLE   I hope not, Niece, for if he does you won't compose your best-loved song. *(he sings)*
    A chantar m'er de ço que non volria ...
    I must sing of what I'd rather not ...

COUNTESS   Oh! That's good. *(sings the rest of the stanza):*
    I'm so angry about him whose friend I am
    for I love him more than anything;
    mercy and courtliness don't help me
    with him, nor does my beauty, or my rank, or my mind...

UNCLE   That's catchy, Niece! I'm sure it will be sung for centuries!   [CURTAIN]

Woman Troubadour

SARAH WHITE

... on mais chan
e pieitz me vai d'amor.

The more I sing, the worse
it goes for me in love.
My Friend carried a glove
beside his skin –
silk, feminine, a Lady's.

I stole it. He said:
'You're pardoned
if you'll sing your song.'

Joy spilled into a canzone:
how I suffered,
all I'd do to gain
a small reward. God!
May it come soon!

He took it in,
taught the song
to his Juggler, then,

sent him off
to one of those estates
whose Lord is always gone –
hunting, whoring, warring –
and the Juggler rattled the gate.
'Come in. Come to my room,'
the Lady cooed,
and handed him a lute.

The Juggler stood in the luster
of the Lady's mirror. A man may sing
a woman's song by switching
here and there an end-word – 'Oh'
for 'Ah.' and vice versa.

Listening,
the Lady paled,
pinked, flamed.

Urgently, she sent for the Juggler's
employer (my Friend) who came
and garnered the reward.
Etcetera. The worse it goes
for me in love, the more I sing.

My name is Alamanda,
Bietris, Carenza,
Gormonda, Ysabella.

I won't grow old. In my whole
life, I'll compose three
perfect songs and lose them all.
I'll shrink into a miniature
red swoop – my gown and hood.

My pen, a centimeter.
My eye, a dot, period

The Cruise

RACHEL HADAS

We put to sea again with our broken oars.
– 'Mythistorema', George Seferis

The ship was still becalmed. Or had we barely begun to move? You students and I sat or lounged on the deck, in little clusters – it was hard to maintain distance. Guest lecturers, one or two of them some weeks, clambered out of their mythical lives (their caves beneath the sea, their specialized islands) to visit us and generously shared an hour with us on the deck: Gregory Nagy, Alicia Stallings, Diane Svarlien, and many others. I could only pay them for their time with maple syrup (my parting guest-gift, if they wanted it) from my trees in another state, another country, another life, another age. To pay for time... but maybe time was cheap. Didn't we all have it in abundance? The students, struggling with assignments and deadlines, might have a different take on time from mine. Still, I wasn't paying (or not paying) for time; I was paying, or not, for knowledge. For wisdom.

The lecturers dried themselves in the sun and sat down with us and told us stories, many secondary stories sprouting, ramifying from the one primal story that we'd been sailing through all semester. Some of their stories came from the province of philology, zeroing in on words that chimed with other words and looped into chains of images and ideas. Natasha Bershadsky pointed out to us the twitching feet of the hanged maids, caught like thrushes in a net, and other birds and animals in extremis. Umit Dhuga linked the bow, the lyre, and the loom, all frames with strings, all held in the hand, all requiring practice, skill, and precision to master and use, and all provoking weeping. Diane Svarlien unpacked a couple of similes from Book Five and set us on the scent of more similes. Gregory Nagy answered a question about Calypso by reminding us that her ill-omened name signified covering something with earth: *I will bury you.* Some of the speakers stood back and looked at bigger, less literary patterns: of hospitality, of gift-giving, of meat-eating. A.E. Stallings considered the Odyssey as fan fiction – meet your favorite heroes again, in the underworld! See (but don't try to embrace) the holograms of the people you knew in life! Moira Egan offered a crown of sonnets spoken, as if in group therapy, by the various naughty ladies, as she called them, in the Odyssey.

We listened, entranced. Or at least I was entranced – how can one ever speak for one's students? All these guests were my friends, from various layers of my now long and deep past life, who gifted us with their knowledge and asked nothing in return. So there we sat – you, my students, and I, eyes fixed on a horizon too far and vague to make out exactly where the sea ended and the sky began.

A student in my other class, someone who rarely spoke, had captured with elegant economy the mood, the weather, the condition, of the time we're living through: 'The pandemic,' she'd blogged, 'has made all our lives blurry.' We closed our blurry eyes, or at least I did, and faced the westering sun. The class nominally met in the mornings; but don't stories begin, if not at bedtime, then at least in the afternoon, as shadows begin to lengthen and the scene, even if only the sea and sky, offers a promise if not of resolution then at least of change? Besides, who at this point could distinguish morning from afternoon? It was hard enough to tell the difference between one day and another.

Walt Whitman wasn't here with us on deck – or was he? Here are his words in 'Crossing Brooklyn Ferry' about the strangely, unbounded world he sensed as he crossed the East River in 1855, in the same state of unboundedness we find ourselves in: 'It avails not, time nor place, distance avails not,/I am with you, you men and women of a generation, or ever so many generations hence...'. It's the very vagueness of temporal boundaries that seems to abolish space and let everyone in. Or else it's zoom technology. Or both. And that vagueness provides its own kind of consolation, its own special encouragement of undreamed-of possibilities.

Because I was a teacher – wait. I hadn't exactly studied or learned to be a teacher, except by teaching for an alarming number of years. And teaching was in my blood, ran in my family – my father, mother, brother, niece – as surely as cheating and mendacity run in Odysseus's family from Autolycus, or even Sisyphus, all the way down to callow Telemachus. But because I was a teacher and you were my students, the thing to do after every guest lecture was to elicit questions. Although come to think of it, when I hear or read a good story, I'm apt to find that questions, if any, come later. First I usually want to lie down and think, or sleep, or cry, or at least leave the crowded room and take a walk. But there were no more crowded rooms now. Even our little class was able to group together on the deck only by the dream dispensation of technology. And no one was allowed to leave the ship unless they leaped into the water.

Each lecturer faded magically back into their illegible life, and we sailed on. Sailed; sail. Were we beginning to move, or was it only an illusion? The bag of winds was tightly stoppered. Is; was. Watch your verb tenses, I always tell my students. Use the present tense when you're writing about literature; stories, on the other hand, narratives of something that happened to you, usually do better in the past tense. Usually – but the narrative of this cruise? Maybe not so past. Maybe eternal present. On we go.

So (having digressed, as old professors do) I elicited questions, as teachers are supposed to. And you, like the dutiful students most of you are, cooperated. Why doesn't god X just kill mortal Y and get it over with? How much power do the gods have, and what are the limits of their power? And then the thorny issues of fidelity, adultery, gender politics, the overwhelming problem of fate – what about all these?

Your questions floated in the chat, in the salty air, and drifted out to sea. No wind. There was no knowing. The lecturer fell silent. So did we. The lecture was over, the class was over, the semester was almost over. Maybe the pandemic was almost over. There was no knowing.

And the story? Salty, deep, unfathomably old, the story had no need of listeners but, wave-like, rolled on and on.

Except that that's not true. Stories need listeners to stay alive. Doesn't the story tell us that the dead must drink warm blood before they speak? And also we all need stories- I do, and you, Tyrese, you, Janel, you, John, you, Blessing, you, Karin, you, Chris L .and Chris J. You need stories, and also you have, are living in and through, your own individual stories. And you and you and you. I hope you will remember this story in the future (the future? Another problematic verb tense) as it retells itself, unspools itself, through you. The story of the Odyssey and of our cruise through it. After the cruise is over. After the ship has docked.

No wind but breath. No harbor, no homecoming – not now, not yet. In our wake, the foam splashed and dissolved. You looked at one another and then at me and then we all turned our faces toward the invisible horizon and thought our private thoughts, perhaps about those strange twins the past and the future, and perhaps about the idea of home.

Letter from Wales

SAM ADAMS

For many years we spent a few weeks each summer in France. We took the car and drove as interest or whim prompted, over several days, to an arranged destination on the Côte d'azur. There we would spend a week before heading back to the channel ferry port by a different leisurely route. On our arrival in France, at the first opportunity, I would seek out a *librairie* and buy a book, hoping that reading would get my mind into gear to meet linguistic challenges ahead. I doubt it ever did that, the French I retained from Aber days having largely declined to the passive sort (though a few glasses of wine were known to stimulate both memory and fluency), but from time to time I picked up a paperback that gave me much more. So it was I chanced upon Alain-Fournier's *Le Grand Meaulnes*, a book and an author that have haunted me for decades since.

Earlier this summer I came upon David Arkell's *Alain-Fournier: A Brief Life* (1986). The sub-title carries a weighty burden of meaning, for the book is a particularly fine account of a life of vivid engagement with the world brutally cut short. Since Alain-Fournier was an admirer of Laforgue, it is entirely fitting that an advertisement on the dust jacket of the biography prompted me to seek out *Looking for Laforgue* (1979) and, as one thing leads to another, I found myself drawn to David Arkell and his own story, which includes being caught by the German advance across France in 1940 and interned for the duration of the war. Briefly, I was hooked. So to Arkell's delightful *Ententes Cordiales* (1989) a collection of his pieces exploring cross-channel mostly literary connections, many originally published in *PN Review*.

All three books are in Carcanet's back catalogue – a triskellion ornament of the press – but it was the Laforgue, an absorbing biographical treatment of another shockingly abbreviated life, that held me. As a French speaker and one who had lived and worked as a journalist in France for a decade, Arkell had no need of an external stimulus to set him on his pursuit of this subject. Nevertheless, I wondered whether he had been prompted or informed by the pioneering essay on Laforgue in Arthur Symons', *The Symbolist Movement in Literature*, which I read in a new Carcanet edition (2014). Originally published in 1899, it had profoundly influenced the young T.S. Eliot, for whom it was 'a revelation' and 'more important for my development than any other book'. In it Symons gathers essays originally published in journals like the *Fortnightly Review* and the *Saturday Review* a year or so earlier, when he was in his early thirties.

I was intrigued to find Arthur Symons was born in Wales – in 1865, at Milford Haven. His relationship to the land of his birth is tenuous, a fact to be recorded in census returns, but without influence on his life thereafter. In the semi-autobiographical 'A Prelude to a Life', that prefaces his collection of stories, *Spiritual Adventures* (1905), he writes, 'I left the place where I was born when I was one year old, and I have never seen it since.' This came about because his father, Mark Symons, born 1824 in the parish of St Columb Minor, Cornwall, was a Wesleyan Methodist minister and subject to 'stationing', that is, placement in a succession of widely scattered churches. That one was over the Bristol Channel might have raised an eyebrow, but South Pembrokeshire's 'little England' would have posed no language problems. In 1853, the Reverend Mark had married Lydia Pascoe (born 1829). She was the daughter of William Pascoe, a farmer of 200 acres in Lower Helland, Bodmin, clearly a family of some substance. The couple met because the

Pascoe family, too, was Wesleyan Methodist, the connexion being particularly strong in Cornwall. Lydia knew what to expect: a peripatetic life, which in their case also included brief halts in St Ives, Exeter, Wellington, Yeovil, Bideford, Leamington, Buckingham, and doubtless other places, town and country, even when her husband was appointed circuit superintendent. He was well-respected and well-liked by his congregations (a local newspaper recorded one made him a gift of forty-five sovereigns), but his only son complained he had never known what it was to have a 'home' and, while he was close to his mother, of his father observed, 'we had nothing akin, he never interested me … If to be good was to be like him, I did not wish to be good.'

Arthur Symons' education was disrupted by movement and incomplete. He claimed he had not learned to read properly until he was nine, never matriculated and did not go to university, but he was a formidable autodidact and linguist. At the publication date of *Spiritual Adventures* he was a poet and dramatist and among the foremost literary critics of the age, with an extraordinary circle of close acquaintance among writers and artists in France and Italy – and Wales. The Welsh connection was re-established by Ernest Rhys, a driving force behind J.M. Dent's vast Everyman Library. Rhys, born 1859 in London, was another autodidact. Symons toured France with the notorious Havelock Ellis; with Rhys he went to Wales, which was probably a quieter experience.

There was a more personal connection. Born in Islington in 1859, Rhys had spent his early childhood in Carmarthen, where his father managed a Gilbey's wine shop. A free run of his grandfather's bookshop in the town gave the boy a voracious appetite for reading, but his formal education, too, was a fractured affair. A brief, unhappy sampling of English grammar schooling at Bishop's Stortford, home of his maternal grandfather, was topped-up at Newcastle-upon-Tyne, where his father's trade had taken the family. He spurned the opportunity of going up to Oxford, choosing instead apprenticeship in mining engineering, which led to employment in the Durham coalfield, all the while pursuing his own route through an expansive literary self-education. In 1886, fired with the ambition to be a writer, he quit the coal industry and headed for London. It was, however, a Newcastle publisher, Walter Scott, who gave him a start, with a commission to edit *The Poems of George Herbert* (1885) and soon after appointed him editor of the Camelot Classics series. In 1891, he married Grace Little from Roscommon in Ireland, whom he had met at the London home of W.B. Yeats, and it was the Rhys's young daughter Megan, at a similar literary gathering, who introduced Arthur Symons to Rhoda Bowser (born 1874), an aspiring actress from a Newcastle-upon-Tyne (again) ship-owning family: they married in 1901. Correspondence, now in America, suggests they shared a warmly affectionate relationship, but they lived much of the time apart, he on extended tours of the continent, or writing at home in rural Kent, while she pursued from a flat in London, and with diminishing success, a career on the stage.

Arthur Symons was a well-known and important figure in literature, the theatre and the arts when, on a visit to Italy in 1908, he suffered a catastrophic nervous collapse, which led to hospitalisation and subsequently, on his return to England, many months in an asylum. It is clear from brief newspaper reports that it was widely thought he was suffering from 'general paralysis of the insane', a consequence of syphilis, and soon to die. It was not syphilis; he survived. The 1911 Census finds Arthur and Rhoda Symons at Island Cottage, Wittersham, Kent, with a male nurse and a domestic servant in attendance. He recovered and began writing and publishing again, but without the same impact as previously. Perhaps his critical grasp of the literary moment had gone, or quite simply times had changed. Rhoda died in 1936, Arthur in 1948. Ernest Rhys, as general editor of Everyman, 'the largest library of cheaply-priced books in the history of publishing before the advent of Penguin', saw 938 titles through the press before he died in May 1946.

Four Poems

CARL PHILLIPS

Fall Colors

I've been looking hard at all my friendships – all of them together,
and each on its own – and although they feel real enough, from what
I can tell, on both sides, I understand now that what they have in common
is a lack of warmth and compassion; who can say at this point why that is,
or how it matters now, if it does. I say I understand it, but it's more true
to say I've *come* to understand it, having had it pointed out to me, for no
reason that I remember, by the only man I think I've ever loved absolutely,
and still do. That's a separate thing. Like my fear of fire. Or like how
much of my time I spend pretending I'm *not* afraid, negotiating this life
with all the seeming casualness with which a man whose business involves
the handling of fires daily

                       daily handles a fire. Some days, it works: I
almost believe myself, or more precisely, and more disturbingly, if I really
think about it (Don't think about it), I almost believe in the self that's just
an imitation of a self I want others to believe in enough for me eventually
to believe it too. Believing in, versus believing...The trumpet vine that grows
up the gingko's trunk and has even reached its branches is an example of
instinct, not affection. Twice a day, instead of walking, I take my dog for
what I call a ramble, where each corner we turn feels like a turning, as well,
of imagination. The sun's behind us now; its heat, on this cold November
afternoon that'll soon join all the rest whose details I've forgotten, seems
a small encouragement: all that's needed, most times. I stop; the dog stops –
our shadows, too. They bloom our shadows north-northeast in front of us.

Scattered Snows, to the North

Does it matter that the Roman
Empire was still early in its slow
unwinding into never again? Then,
as now, didn't people burst into tears
in front of other people, or in private,
for no reason that they were willing
to give, or they weren't yet able to,

or for just no reason? I've never
stopped missing you, I used to
practice saying, for when I'd
need those lines, as I assumed
I would, given what I knew then –
nothing, really – about things
like love, trust, the betrayal
of trust, and a willfulness that's
only deepened inside me, all
these years, during which I can
almost say I've missed no one –
though it hurts,
                    to say it...

Honestly, the Roman Empire,
despite my once having studied it,
barely makes any sense to me now,
past the back-and-forthing of
patrolled borders as the gauge
and proof of hunger's addictive
and erosive powers. But there were
people, of course, too, most of them
destined to be unremembered,
who filled in their drawn lives
anyway – because what else
is there? – to where the edges
gave out. If it was night, they lit
fires, presumably. Tears
were tears.

Heroic Interval

Up from the bottom of wherever in the mind things go
to be forgotten, most of them forever, he reappears
at the edge of that meadow inside me I've spent
most of my life trying to convince others isn't made up
at all, but real. As

                    he was. Is. Above him, a bewilderment
of black swans pulling their bodies across a band
of nightfall, though it can't be night, for the meadow's
not dark yet, it keeps flashing like a basin of water set down

                    *

in sunlight. As he walks towards me, it almost looks
like the routine gesture with interruptions that I
used to think love more or less came down to, before I
figured out I could stop –

                    I could always have stopped –
and should maybe try to. Closer, now. He parts the grasses,
breast-high, in front of him. His arms like blades
meant for winnowing intimacy from tenderness, or

                    *

nostalgia from truth. Nothing's changed. Still the kind
of man who sees no reason to take his gloves off –
assassin gloves – during sex. Still a kind of dream,
that moment in dream when a friend whom you've
learned not to trust entirely

                    slowly turns to tell you –
half threatening it, half consolation – the only dream
is this one. But it isn't a dream – I can tell. He'd be
taking his gloves off. He'd be raising his soft hands
to his face – scorched map; busted compass. He'd have a face.

Rehearsal

By then the point of the forest was the getting through it.
Then it lay behind them, all but its sharper details – flies licking at
dried blood, I think, on a random tree stump – getting swiftly lost,
its muffled birdsong, too, that had come less, it seemed, from
the trees than from beneath, mostly, as if somewhere deep,
deep inside the earth. What if meeting you has been
the one good reason I lasted so long in a world that must
eventually not include me, I almost said to him. Past the forest,

the shore, where the land ended, where briefly the waves hitting it
seemed the latest example of how squandering momentum can
become routine; while, upon the waves, the taken-for-grantedness
of shadowplay seemed its own example: how one way to prove power
can be to quietly assume it. Then except for offshore, where the dark lay
like – defiantly – a ship at anchor, everything was itself. As it always
had been. They took off their shoes, their clothes.
They swam out to the dark ship.

The Bureaucratic Sublime

On the Secret Joys of Contemporary Poetry

ALEX WYLIE

Since the untimely death of David Graeber, a year ago at the time of writing, I have been looking once more through his catalogue of work: a catalogue, leaving the many articles and essays aside, which includes such brilliant, mind-altering books as *Debt: The First Five Thousand Years*; *Bullshit Jobs: A Theory* (a real life-ring, this one was, when I first read it in 2018); and, perhaps my favourite, *The Utopia of Rules: On Technology, Stupidity, and the Secret Joys of Bureaucracy*. These are all books that, if not necessarily that cliché of 'changing my life', I think made my life seem more valid: they suggested that, perhaps, I wasn't *completely* losing my grip, and was not as isolated as I felt. In the more circumspect mood in which I re-read his work after his death, *The Utopia of Rules*, with its account of the bureaucratic as cultural-political paradigm, seemed even more urgent and timely beyond its personal appeal to me; and it has prompted me to consider its connections to the poetry of this current, bureaucratic, paradigm. Its point for political ideology as for poetry (and of much of Graeber's work) is, I think, that what the citizens of the freedom-advertising democracies of the West *really* desire, or are made to desire, is freedom from freedom itself. This is what the bureaucratic, considered in its broader and deeper dimensions, affords the citizens of liberal democracies; it is the utopian form of our various dystopias, the waking dream of freedom underpinned by the secret joys of a commodious, but guiltless, unfreedom.

In *The Utopia of Rules*, then, Graeber defines the current political era as 'the age of total bureaucratization'. Neoliberalism, despite its overt ideology of deregulation and (vaguely defined) personal and public freedoms, breeds ever more bureaucracy, says Graeber; and with this bureaucratic proliferation comes inevitably 'a timid, bureaucratic spirit' which 'has come to suffuse every aspect of intellectual life' and which, crucially, 'comes cloaked in a language of creativity, initiative, and entrepreneurialism'. In other words, the contemporary political moment, in the UK and USA especially, is characterised by a loss of agency, across a number of interconnected spheres, ideologically cloaked as an unprecedented upsurge in personal agency. In *Against Creativity*, Oli Mould provides a view of this contemporary inversion: '[b]eing creative in today's society has only one meaning: to carry on producing the status quo'. Creativity, in this argument, has become a counter-progressive power dressed up, of necessity, as progressive.

So, for Graeber and others, bureaucracy and creativity are intertwined in our cultural-political moment. We may be in an age in which the notion of individual creativity is an archaism (as Marjorie Perloff has claimed) but that very notion is the ideological fantasy fuelling the increasing bureaucratisation of our lives. This 'bureaucratic spirit', as Graeber puts it, offers freedom from risky and chaotic creativity into the purer (and probably more lucrative) pleasures of the 'creative'; a guiltless reduction into ever more commodious, though alienated, forms of social existence. Neoliberal risk-aversion and procedure are elevated into cultural paradigm, offering within the Creative Industries, for example, the opportunity to be 'a creative' (a status as indefinite as its indefinite article suggests). Being *a* creative liberates you yet further from the chaotic and dangerous actualities of creativity, empowering you to dream of the endless potentials of self-creation. Administration has become creativity, and vice versa. On social media, for instance, people have the power to 'curate' and 'develop' their identities, their fingerprint on social reality; or, from another point of view, these platforms have made even humanity in its most intimate social forms a cynosure of regulation. The secret joy of social media is, indeed, being mediated at the most intimate social levels, like a sort of consensual panopticon. This sort of secret joy is what I'm calling here the bureaucratic sublime.

And this is a twenty-first-century mirror-image of the Romantic sublime. 'Poetry puts a spirit of life and motion into the universe', writes William Hazlitt in *Lectures on the English Poets*. The bureaucratic sublime (similarly vaguely – and the sublime always depends on vagueness for its power) offers the prospect of 'a spirit of life and motion', but supplemented by a profound, secret joy arising from freedom from these very conceptual forces. 'What ultimately lies behind the appeal of bureaucracy is fear of play', as Graeber puts it, elsewhere describing 'a tacit cosmology in which the play principle (and by extension, creativity) is itself seen as frightening, while game-like behaviour is celebrated as transparent and predictable, and where, as a result, the advance of all these rules and regulations is itself experienced as a kind of freedom.' A recent review by Fiona Sampson of Rachel Boast's *Hotel Raphael* epitomises this spirit:

> Her markedly old-fashioned literary sensibility, informed by Romanticism even, sometimes leads to a little too much fine writing. But the slightly suffocating inwardness is redeemed by the force of poems such as 'Hand, Match, Ashtray', which address a chronic health condition with fierceness and delicacy. (*Guardian*, 14/5/21)

'[O]ld-fashioned literary sensibility' is equated here with 'fine writing', the readership of the *Guardian* assumed by Dr Sampson to be part of this culture of self-consolation in which poetic style, or 'literary sensibility', is pegged as suffocatingly inward. The in-group of the

Guardian's review pages is presumably more at home with a poem addressing a 'chronic health condition'. Dr Sampson's use of 'fine' modulates into the laudatory, however, when talking about subject matter, describing Martina Evans's 'finely perceptive poems about houses and families'. In true bureaucratic spirit, subject matter rules here; style is an ideological embarrassment. Subject matter (or 'content') can be easily assessed, described, and categorised; style cannot. This contemporary promotion of the generic goes hand in hand, then, with a political culture of funding allocations and professional reward: the 'language of creativity, initiative, and entrepreneurialism'. The readers of the *Guardian* are allowed, in a pact of tacit understanding, to share the denigration of 'fine writing' whilst approving the easy descriptions of subject matter.

'Fine' is a word with a broad range of meaning – an ideal word for such ideological disavowals. Fiona Sampson's dispraise of 'fine writing' encompasses various meanings offered by the *OED*: 'apposite, well expressed'; 'affecting refinement or elegance'; 'affectedly or excessively elaborate'; whereas her praise of 'finely perceptive poems about houses and family' may suggest the more materialistic 'of a tool or point, having a sharp edge or point'. Such a utilitarian emphasis may be apt to an age of democratic materialism, as Alain Badiou has described it; perhaps a poem which is 'about' things, say a house or a family, is felt to have more of an 'edge' and certainly more of a 'point' to it. As the Creative Industries Council informs us, 'The economic impact of the UK's arts and culture industry is *quantified* in a report which highlights the sector's high productivity and effect on employment.' (Creative Industries Council website, 3/6/21: italics mine.) Subject matter is readily described in, transcribed into, the terms of this bureaucratic political culture. Poetic style, however, is precisely that which is untranslatable, resistant to quantification. This is why in contemporary poetry there is such an emphasis on subject matter, on poems *about* subjects: 'health conditions', tales of houses and families, and so on. This is a poetry of the quantifiable, in which poetry proliferates, just as creativity proliferates, as a marketable social good. It is the American Dream in Received Pronunciation.

There is a very famous passage in which the 'fine' is considered as a characteristic of the poet: that is, the almost-proverbial speech by Duke Theseus in Shakespeare's *A Midsummer Night's Dream*:

The poet's eye in a fine frenzy rolling
Doth glance from heaven to earth, from earth to
   heaven;
And as imagination bodies forth
The form of things unknown, the poet's pen
Turns them to shape, and gives to airy nothing
A local habitation and a name.

Chosen by Arts Council England as an official quotation for a recent National Poetry Day, this passage seems to be the go-to statement, in English-language literature, anyway, on the poetic or creative imagination. The Duke's use of 'fine' here, retroactively, unites the bifurcation of sense in Dr Sampson's usage, of fine as 'elaborate and affected', even as 'empty rhetoric' (*OED* definition 12), and as 'having a sharp edge or point', as well as other approbatory connotations – even 'pure; perfect'. The image of the poet's 'fine frenzy' may now be dominated by such definitions of fineness as 'suffocating inwardness', which was no doubt part of Shakespeare's intention, speaking through his character (himself a kind of journalistic pundit here) – but, crucially, only part of it. While the act itself may be described, pejoratively, as 'fine', the product of the creative act is what the Duke (and Shakespeare?) *really* wants to eulogise here. While the act of creativity, and the creator, might be subject to caricature, it is art itself which does the caricaturing.

Prompted by this passage, we might say, also, that there may well be something faintly traumatic, or at the very least *awkward*, about the work of art. Perhaps this quality is what defines the work of art as such – a perception that drives Denise Riley's poetry, for example ('Out of | the depth of its shame it starts singing'). The uncompromising compromises us. However, whereas the event, in philosophical vocabulary, is the inevitable thing which could not have been foreseen – 'The form of things unknown' – the bureaucratic thrives by foreseeing all and making the future as inevitable as possible. Nothing is more threatening to capital than risk (an element which is, in another beautiful ideological disavowal, fundamentally constitutive of it). Bureaucracy muffles the traumatic, deletes the awkward; it is all about smooth flow, maintained systems, eliminated risk; and, accordingly, the bureaucratic emphasis is on creativity itself, rather than on the productions of creativity. People participate in this bureaucratic culture because they are encouraged to see themselves as *anti*-bureaucratic – as embodying the kind of 'spirit' defined by Hazlitt, the 'spirit of life and motion' we see now in advertising: 'Catch that Pepsi spirit'; 'Coke adds life'; 'Hugo Boss: Boss in motion'. It is a creativity liberated from risks to health – Diet Creativity, you might say.

Style and matter are always in some kind of balance, and perhaps in Shakespeare and Thomas Nashe in the 1590s, for instance, that balance upends at times toward an apotheosis of style – though with this apotheosis usually goes a certain self-consciousness, an ironic attitude toward rhetoric's temptations. But contemporary English-language poetry is currently tipping over into a prevalence of matter, reflecting, among other things, a (superficially 'democratic materialist') attitude that literature exists to reflect its social and historical moment (a tendency reflected also in the increasing prevalence of social sciences in university-level literary studies and in literary 'theory'). The dividing line between an ethically, politically driven 'anti-style' tendency and a social-media-driven 'linguistic timorousness' (recently described by Emma Dabiri in the excellent *What White People Can Do Next*) is accordingly a thin one. Poetry-prize culture is symptomatic of the bureaucratic spirit, in which poetry is addressed to judges themselves beholden to state-bureaucratic forces, as is the system of rewarding prize-winners with lucrative academic posts; and this situation speaks also to the erosion of a 'reading public' for poetry, suggestive of the situation we have now in which readers of poetry are themselves part of the ever-expanding landscape of the creative industries of which poetry is increasingly a feature.

In a time of political foment and genuinely progressive moments and movements, it is natural and desirable that poetry, and all other cultural forms, reflect that foment, express it and in some way crystallise and embody it. It is important to remember in the case of poetry, however, that style and form are not only operative in the art-form but operative in its cultural-political reactions and assertions. Poetic style and form can themselves be reflexes of cultural, political, social assertion, and not trivial ones in the context of artistic 'action'. It is as if achievement in artistic form, specifically here poetic form, voice, style, etc., offers dissent *per se* – in a more *universal*, yet still *material*, sense – rather than dissent in a particular cause. The fact that this dissent cannot be defined in particular terms is itself in the nature of the dissent. The detail and nuance that these things embody constitute a kind of freedom, a freedom as burdensome, as heuristic, as freedom really is – the kind acknowledged by the dictum that 'pedantry is freedom' – but also in the sense that attention to form, style, voice, and so on, keeps the poet 'honest' even as it propels her into artifice, pushing her beyond the prescribed boundaries of her accepted and acceptable idioms. The advice to 'write about what you know' sounds superficially quite sensible, until you consider the cultural-political situation this offers in which no one says anything unknown, in which the unknown as such becomes disapproved of. The authentic and the progressive thus become intertwined with the inauthentic and the regressive – a negation characterising our age.

The crisis I have been describing in this essay lies in no small part in creativity now being promoted as universally attainable. Of course, at some level, everyone can be creative, but at the same level this is a fairly meaningless assertion. Government rhetoric abounds with these kinds of idioms, as does advertising. While many things *should* be universally attainable – and Universal Basic Income is being trialled in Wales as I write, a good example of this kind of universal access to social goods – artistic creativity never can be and, crucially, perhaps never should be. Creativity is now seen as this kind of social good, but this seems fatally off-beam, to me; surely, it is the productions of creativity which are the social good, a position which, as I've suggested, Duke Theseus (and Shakespeare?) might seem to have agreed with. The promotion of creativity as a social good – you might say a kind of democratic privilege – is characteristic, rather, of the neoliberal bureaucratic spirit, its false empowerments and consumer-psychologist propaganda. The logic is that of the pseudo-progressive advertising tagline: 'unlock the creative potential in YOU!' But what's really being sold is not creativity, as such, but 'being creative': that is, lifestyle rather than power, lifestyle which can only be sold in the guise of power. The secret joy this freedom from freedom provides is what I'm calling the bureaucratic sublime: it is neoliberalism's liberation from liberation itself. In this age of democratic materialism, then, it would be an ironic triumph (and fit monument to his memory) if, as David Graber puts it at the end of *The Utopia of Rules*, we were able 'to let our imaginations once again become a material force in human history'.

Montpeyroux Sonnets (2)

MARILYN HACKER

A rainy Monday, everything is shut.
It could be late October; it's mid-May.
Lights on at noon, outside, rain drums on gray
paving stones, drainpipes, voices. Nothing but
water on roof tiles in a steady beat,
the postman's motorcycle passing by,
not stopping. Tomorrow, the bakery,
grocer, butcher – bread, vegetables, meat,
revivifying possibility
of a 'bonjour' exchanged with an unknown
person, whose eyes express the smile,
question, mistrust or curiosity
her or his face mask almost hides, as I
exhale uneasily behind my own.

Exhale uneasily. Behind my own
pretense of standing firmly, I'm unsteady
on my feet, impatient but unready
to take one more step, toward some overgrown
weed-wilded plot. Leaden feet weigh me down
on the empty morning street. Ahead, I
see the post office, clock tower. I buy bread. I
buy a bunch of red onions. The town
is quiet as the plague that got its claws
into the blue-green globe a year ago.
Queasily accustomed to the laws
that change monthly, the shops shuttered because...
I make my way, awkwardly lame and slow,
up sloping streets out of DiChirico

Up sloping streets out of DiChirico,
too clean, too empty, garrulous grans indoors,
kids quiet, holiday-rental visitors
quarantined in cities , the status quo
is stasis. Now, here, stays here and now:
curfew, a trajectory that blurs
the border of the ten kilometres
allowed beyond the door. Today, tomorrow,
something will change, the wind, the rules, the weather,
a numbness, swelling , or suspicious cough.
Yesterday, in late sunlight, on an off-
road, a brown horse stood in a field,
flanks aglow in the slant light , untethered
and shimmering in a stasis that seemed wild.

Shimmering in a stasis that seems wild,
unseasonable, unpredictable
as thunderstorms or canicule in April,
the certainty of change . There was a tiled
corridor; the amputated, undefiled
torso of a boy in stippled marble;
a bird that cawed, that whistled, one that warbled;

a sketch of an old man reading, sketch of a child
herself bending to draw a hopscotch grid
near the gazebo on the village square.
I sat on a bench there. I thought of Claire
eighty-two years ago – a similar
village, the same grid, during the drôle de guerre,
not thinking she'd write about it. But she did.

Not thinking he'd write about it, still, he did,
first scribbling birdtracks on a yellow lined
pad – place-names, objects left behind,
in his three languages. He stopped in mid-
phrase (they weren't sentences) as a word fled,
or was it the object, shimmering in mind,
but disappearing, shrinking to a blind
spot with a velvet aura. He shook his head,
rubbed his eyes, squinting, put down the pen,
light pricking them like summer dust that stings.
Beyond the window, a street full of things
in motion, even when they were still.
That wasn't the road leading out of Tell
Abyad, that he was walking on again,

Walking out of the ruined town again,
having gone back to probe the rubble, look
for what was left of the school, the mosque, the book-
shop, where after school daily eight or ten
children would awkwardly appear, and listen
to tales they'd coax from him – he shook,
despite himself. Here was the souk,
or had been. No ma'anouche, no heaps of green
and russet vegetables, no polyester
djellabas, no men, no women, no mercantile
palaver, only an urban vacant lot,
cardboard boxes, dogshit, a scrawny cat,
and plastic bags of household trash on piles
on rubble. I'm not him. But I was there.

I'm not there, probing the rubble. I wasn't there
with cousins in Gaza as the bombs
exploded. Israeli bombs. Agents have names.
I'm not holding the pen that doesn't spare
me. No sleep. The pointless vigils wear
me down. Bad back. Bad conscience. Spasms
drizzle and clutch my spine, and open chasms
of half-remembered mishaps, terror, error.
To walk out through the fields was easier
than through damp city streets that probed my pain
(or joy) sometimes, with something to discover,
translate, transform, enumerate again
at every corner bus stop, shop front. But
it's Monday. Almost everything is shut.

Ford, Biala and Politics

MARTIN STANNARD

In the 1929 *Who's Who in Literature*, Ford Madox Ford is sandwiched quietly between William Byron Forbush (author of *The Kindergarten Manual*, 1921), and the Rev. Harold Ford (author of *Art of Extempore Speaking*, then in its 12th edition). If Ford had ever glanced at these entries while checking the proofs of his own, he might have wished for a less confused childhood and envied the Rev. Ford's literary popularity. Ford is listed as the author of twenty-one books, and co-author (with Conrad and Violet Hunt) of another four. He was a major figure of English and American letters, and had had considerable sales over the last fourteen years with *The Good Soldier* and the *Parade's End* tetralogy, but none of his works had run to twelve editions, and he was about to plunge off the cliff of recent success with the Wall Street Crash and alimony. His address is given as South Lodge, 80 Campden Hill Road, London, W.8., the house he had shared with Hunt. That was long out of date. Since then, indeed since 1919, he had been living with Stella Bowen, the Australian painter, in England, Paris, Cap Ferrat and Toulon, and they had had his third child, Julia, in 1920. It was when Julia was just two that Ford and Stella had decamped to France. He had, in effect, been on the run from the previous women in his life since deserting his wife, Elsie Martindale, and their two daughters, during 1909.

By the time we pick up the story here, on 1 May 1930, Ford was based in Paris, and his social reputation was in ruins. Separated from Stella, making serious love (in the Jamesian sense) to a married American heiress after his disastrous affair with Jean Rhys, he found himself sitting on a sofa in his studio between two beautiful young women. It was one of his 'Thursdays', when he (and previously Stella) would open their apartment to friends for drinks and dancing to the gramophone. Ford liked to dance, and although he was clumsy, gained immense pleasure from it, as he did from hosting parties, playing Patience, looking at paintings, gardening, cooking, smoking, flirting, and music in general. Ezra Pound, his close literary companion, although a tennis player rather than a dancer, would often attend, as he had the 'Tuesdays' at South Lodge. In fact, one of the two young women, Eileen Lake, a poet, had engineered this meeting to talk to Pound, not Ford. But Pound hadn't turned up. She was in Paris with her husband Michael Lake, a doctor, and they had paid for the passage of the other woman, a penniless New York Jewish artist, desperate to taste European culture. In the event, the married couple returned to the States, and their friend stayed in France, making it her home until, after Ford's death in 1939, the German invasion forced her to return to America.

That other woman was the painter Janice Tworkov, then twenty-six years old, who some three months earlier had adopted the name of her birthplace, 'Biala', to distinguish her work from that of her brother Jack.

Her letters to him, to her close friend and fellow artist

Shelby Cox, and to Jack's wife, Wally, offer us a new 'fly-on-the -wall' account of her life with Ford 1930–39, and much more, particularly about politics, the politics of art, and sexual politics. This essay will deal, briefly, with all three as essential ingredients of that long, passionate conversation she had with Ford. At the heart of everything lies the idea of 'culture': the function of the artist in society, and the problems of abstraction and pure form as opposed to social responsibility and representation. Let us start with names and naming.

Janice's letters demonstrate that she had not only fallen in love with Ford but also with France. The bread shops transported her back to her childhood, beyond the poverty and terrible family confusions of her New York life as an adolescent in rough schools, and a struggling art student on the Lower East Side. Until she was ten, she had lived with her family in Biala, a village in occupied Poland. Her father, a tailor to the Russian army, was often away, following the movements of the troops. She recalled happy days exploring the countryside. But, although this was in some ways an age of innocence for her before she became aware of the problems of her parents' marriage, there were already deep cultural confusions. They were Jews living in a gentile area. They couldn't enter the houses of their gentile friends. Some years before her mother, Esther, and the children had immigrated to America in 1913, her father, Herman, had gone on ahead with his mother to set up shop in New York. So for those years, the family in Poland, formerly, it seems, reasonably prosperous, were plunged into penury, trying to eke out a living from whatever Herman could send back and whatever he had saved. Even those simple terms 'the family' and 'the children' were complicated. Both parents had brought considerable psychological baggage to their union. Esther had divorced a man she loved passionately because he could not give her children. Herman, a widower, came to Esther with five children in search of a mother. Then there were Herman and Esther's parents. So the 'family' was eleven, not four, all of whom appear to have lived in New York in one room behind the shop. It was good to be reunited but it came at a formidable price. Esther was a loveless mother, even to her natural children. She lived out a long nervous breakdown, always regretting her divorce, while Herman, gentle and supportive, tried unsuccessfully to see her through it. Culturally they were orthodox Jews who stuck together in times of trouble. But who were they? What were their names? When were they born? Where did they belong?

As Jack explained, '[...] I left Poland Jakov Tworkovsky and arrived Jacob Bernstein.' Along the way he was 'Jake' to those American relatives who had preceded his family to Ellis Island, then 'Jacob', then Jack. These relatives had all taken the name 'Bernstein' to 'prove' blood relation to other immigrant relatives sponsoring them. The same thing happened with Jack's family. His parents remained

Bernsteins while he and his sister reclaimed their original name in their naturalisation papers, shortening it to 'Tworkov'. But neither knew exactly when they were born or where. 'No small part of being an immigrant was that in coming from Poland to America, we not only crossed several frontiers, but several centuries. I could not have grown up in this country without being reborn. There is therefore a period in my early life which has in some sense fallen off me like a dead branch, especially that part which *[has meaning* – deleted*]* is merely data.' In an undated typewritten note he added: 'Most people are born with names. I had to acquire one. [...] The name I have finally acquired I have [had] to grow into like a foot into a badly shaped shoe. [...] The messing around with my name was not my doing – it was purely accident. [...] Of the two parts of my present name the one I detest most is the 'Jack.' ' His 'real' name was 'Jankel' 'as my mother and father continued to call me all their living days – God bless their sacred memory.'

Janice did not bless their sacred memory with quite the same fervour. A long letter she wrote to Jack on October 23, 1929 just a day prior to the Wall Street Crash, reads in part:

I got fired at Macey's and realized myself that I don't fit into that sort of thing. Everything in modern business is so standardized that there is no chance for an ordinary human being.

I am painting father right now. He's being 70 in January and they're giving him a party. I hope to sell them the canvas and give him the money.

The situation at home is awful. They persecute me as if I were an early Christian. I don't believe you have any idea what it's really like. They've got me in a state [...] where I'm on the extreme edge of despair Everyone, mother, [...] her children, our dear brothers and sister (these not directly to my face) neighbors, friends, nephews, in short everyone [double underlined] treat me like a piece of rotten fruit because I'm not married yet. And not one of them, whether I know them or not, hesitate to plead with me on the subject. I think if I don't commit suicide out of pure nerves, I will probably die of disgust. All the sensitiveness I had at 15 when I heard our dear brothers tell us stories written about excrement has come back to me.

Recently after an awful blow up, peace was made, and in the first flush of it I let myself be led back to the family. Last night I was at Elia's. Just the noise, and from the 'vulgarity', knocked me out so that I still tremble. My one aim in life is to get away from New York or I swear I'll either go nuts or die. What makes it so awful is that I'm just as ready to dissolve in tears over mother's tragedy as mine.

It's all there: poverty, the problems with her parents and Jewish relations generally, the artistic struggle. But the sense of alienation goes much deeper than feeling depressed by family pressure, and being penniless. She, of course, had suffered the same identity trauma with her name as Jack, was only 'Janice' by self-invention. Originally Schenehaia Tworkovsky, she became Ida Bern-

stein, then Janice Tworkovska, Tworkovsky, Tworkov, evolving through Janice Tworkov or Ford, and choosing 'Biala' as a separate professional moniker. Her parents called her 'Ida'. But Biala (as I shall call her hereafter) lacked Jack's determination to be reborn as an American. In her early days in New York she couldn't rationalise her sense of alienation other than to attribute it to her difficulties with her family, her lovers, acute poverty. As soon as she set foot in Paris, however, all this changed. Suddenly France was where she belonged, and almost immediately she was writing to Jack saying that she intended never to return to the States. 'This country is so damn beautiful it is impossible to think of anything else [...]. I assure you, now that I'm well out of it, America looks more like a stony prison [...].'

It is important to understand the context of Biala's letters to Jack before getting on to her relationship with Ford. Jack and Biala were close but very different characters and artists. As Tworkov's Provincetown neighbour, the poet Stanley Kunitz, remarked: 'Jack took care of everything – his car, his house, his lawn, his tools, his studio, his brushes, his family, himself.'

There is a distinct sense in these letters that she senses his disapproval of her affair with Ford, and that disapproval was complex. It had to do politics: family and cultural politics. We find her saying that he was wrong to regard Europe as a bankrupt culture, that if he would only *try* France she was sure he would love it as much as she. A constant theme is her guilt: guilt at abandoning her first husband, the painter Lee Gatch, and a new lover, Tommy someone, and her starving family; at not having enough money to send anything back, at disappointing her Jewish parents by shacking up with yet another gentile; at not being able to admit that she was shacking up. Even when she was with Ford she had nightmares about her mother beating on the door and finding her living in sin.

She finds herself in those 1930s letters awkwardly balanced between praising the paradisal life of Villa Paul on Cap Brun in Toulon – the food, the wine, the bread, the sunshine and view of the Mediterranean – and stressing that this is only possible because everything is so cheap for her and Ford when living on a dollar a day. There is persistent anxiety about rubbing the faces of her family in the dirt, abandoning them, and it is probable that Jack, much as he loved and missed her, *did* feel that she was being irresponsible, that Ford's celebrity and connections must be bringing in more than she was admitting. On the other hand, he could not take the moral high ground. He was already twice divorced. And when he met Wally in 1932, who was to become his third wife, later the mother of Helen and Hermine, she was only sixteen, he thirty-two. Both were political radicals, socialists, near communists, active in marches and sit-ins. Jack later went on to draw a small income from odd jobs, some teaching, and the Treasury Department's Public Works of Art Project (WPA) as part of the New Deal. But he was pretty well starving when Biala's first letters from France began to arrive, and Ford represented, or seemed to represent, everything he despised: old-school European feudalism, clubmanship, influence, patronage. A famous image of Ford in America during the late 1920s depicted him in top hat and tails, chortling over a cigar like a parody capitalist on a communist propaganda poster.

Her letters are thus difficult to 'read' in that they are trying to please different, sometimes conflicting, expectations to excuse herself from guilt. So when she says that Ford has Jewish relations, she is trying to manufacture a story that will please her parents. And when she says that she is becoming 'violently communistical' and that Ford is, too, she is trying to please Jack. But when she says that it is difficult to be a woman and a foreigner attempting to establish herself as an artist, and complains bitterly about the male-dominated art world, she surely speaks from the heart. That sense of the gender imbalance in the politics of art, of the patronage (the withholding of financial patronage) from women, the talking down, had been there in her earlier New York letters to Jack. Then she had felt anxious about disagreeing with him, especially about Art. She would drag his canvases round snowbound New York streets to exhibitions feeling all the while that he was the better painter, he had accommodated modernist practice better than she, he was the finer critic, the nobler creature, while she was tormented by the idea that she might just be a talentless 'silly girl', making a fuss over nothing.

Between the lines of the 1930s letters, however, another story emerges. Ford gave her the self-confidence she needed to experiment, and here we come to the nature of their love, so strange for others to understand. Ford, too, had had several names: Ford Hueffer, Ford Madox Hueffer or Ford Madox Ford, in addition to his numerous *noms de plume*. There is something of the social chameleon about both of them, camouflaged observers. Both ran under assumed names, flags of convenience. Both wanted to escape their immediate pasts, fly by those nets, and if that involved lying to those wanting to trammel them up in old obligations, so be it. They would even, in a way, harmlessly lie to each other to preserve what they had, or at least to keep quiet. Ford seems never to have discussed with Biala his Catholic conversion, and invented some Jewishness, while at the same time writing to Stella insisting on their daughter's Catholic education. He would say anything to keep Biala, to whom he clutched as to what remained of life itself. It is doubtful whether he ever discussed his marriage to Elsie, his fraught relations with Violet Hunt, Jean Rys, and his heiress. Perhaps Biala just didn't want to know, preferring not to paddle back up the murky waters of her husband's desertions, and hers of Gatch, Tommy and the family. They were here and now, orphans of the storm, washed up together in Paris and making some kind of home furnished with bits and pieces of Louis XIII or Louis XV – a place to work on equal terms beyond the catcalls of the past. He had had a serious heart attack in the late 1920s. They wouldn't have much time together and they determined to make the most of what there was, Miranda and Prospero.

In terms of cultural politics, they came from opposite sides of the border but both shared the sense of immigrant alienation described by Jack. Ford's father was German, then naturalised English, hers either Russian or Polish. Both were politically inclined towards liberalism,

communal living, sharing resources. Ford had flirted with a kind of idealism based on Englishness, the essential decency of the English gentleman, feudalism, all of which had died in the trenches during an apocalyptic capitalist war. But he, although he craved 'respectability', social and professional, had never been able to remain 'respectable' in the old-fashioned sense. His insistence on calling all his partners, even Biala, 'Mrs Ford' had led to scandal and sneering. Biala had found this further re-naming difficult at first. He had done it without consulting her. She was furious when a reviewer of one of her shows described her as 'Janice Ford Biala'. Interviewed by Sondra Stang late in life, however, she saw this as an endearing quirk on his part. The fact that he described all his women as his wife meant that he regarded them as his wife, even though he couldn't marry them. She was in no doubt. He was a feminist long before his time.

This might seem an odd description of a man seen by a hoard of catcallers to be pompous, autocratic to the point of being 'baronial'; a man who left many women, and who might have seemed almost to have flirted himself to death. But there was another way of reading him: Biala's way and, for a long time, Violet Hunt's and Stella's. This presented an image of a gentle and caring man, fiercely defensive of women's rights but profoundly uncertain of himself. His charm, his courtliness, his dancing were not the armoury of the lady-killer but quite the reverse: a sensitivity to those who felt disempowered, a drawing of them out, a giving of confidence. Thus the three elements of politics mentioned earlier – governmental, cultural, and sexual – combined in him to make him almost irresistible to a female artist in the 1930s. He was a conservative anarchist, leaning leftwards; he was an experimental artist himself with many connections to Modernist writers and painters, and he was a feminist who saw it as his business to lend collaborative strength, confidence, to his female friends.

This question of lending strength is an interesting, and knotty, one. Biala was determined to make her own way, to stand up to the male establishment and outface it with her own merits. But she was for a long time uncertain of these merits, and she had to deal in her epistolary discussions with Jack with his prejudices against Ford. When Jack's wife Wally went with Ford and Biala to Benfolly the antebellum home of Allen Tate and Caroline Gordon in Clarksville, Tennessee, to act as Ford's secretary, Jack saw the whole Southern feudal culture, the Agrarian 'thing', as a nonsense based quietly on the idea of slavery and autocracy. His sister, he thought, was 'silly' for falling for it. 'I imagine in the south', he wrote to Wally in 1937, 'if three cultured people get together they must feel extra special cultured. Is it true? Or am I prejudiced? Of course my idea of culture and Ford's, say, is so different. And you know what I mean. As long as the south is the most reactionary sore spot and threat against the entire country how could these people talk of culture.'

Jack used the term 'culture' in the sense that Raymond Williams later used it in *Culture and Society 1780–1950* (1958). Both rejected the defence of the 'high' culture of Europe so often advocated by artists like Henry James, T.S. Eliot, Pound, and, until he met Biala, Ford himself.

Oddly, this had become the baseline of arguments about cultural politics for many Anglophone literary Modernists. 'Culture' to Jack was the complex intertwining of all social systems, it described a whole way of life in whatever social strata. But what he could not see, and Biala could, was that Ford had cast himself out of the gentlemanly club, or been cast out from it, and had lost his faith in it during his time on the Western Front. He was as anti-fascist as Jack, as protective of the Jews suffering under Hitler and Mussolini as Biala. 'Culture' to him was artistry, whoever produced it, and he saw the Provence of the Troubadors (on whom his father had written the definitive nineteenth-century book) as at the heart of the whole project. A great culture cherished its artists above all other citizens. In this, often apolitical, historical context Ford had become what now seems like a 'new man': a 'green', promoting the 'small producer', living off the land; a great cook; a feminist. He had been all these things before the First World War but in the role of gentleman smallholder. What had changed was that he had become, been forced to become by the financial collapse of 1929 and the demands of alimony, a bohemian. It was this Ford that Biala loved.

When his father had died in his forties, Ford was still a child. Ford's maternal grandfather, the Pre-Raphaelite painter Ford Madox Brown, had taken him, his brother and their mother in, and instilled in the boys, as well as his huge intellectual range and great kindness, an essential principle. The great mass of people, sympathetic as he felt towards the ideas of his socialist friend William Morris, Madox Brown regarded as merely 'the stuff to fill graveyards'. The most important beings, he insisted, were artists. Art was the life-blood of any culture, without which there was mere materiality and the mortmain of 'facts'. Ford lived by this edict all his life, and in Biala he at last found a fellow traveller. Obsessively driven by their muse, both demanded the freedom to revision the world through a shifting landscape of impressions rather than the analysis of data. And so they lived shiftlessly together between Paris, Toulon, and America for the nine years until he collapsed in her arms on the boat back to France from America, an improbable, penniless couple perfectly content in each others' company. As a boy, Ford had modelled William Tell's son for his grandfather, staring innocently at the viewer, holding the two halves of the apple that had been shot from his head. In retrospect this image seems symbolic of the cultural schizophrenia that characterised Ford's mind as an artist. Biala, perhaps, helped him to reunite the two halves of that apple, restoring to him a kind of innocence and psychological unity. He did much the same for her.

from 'Ungovernable Bodies'

JEE LEONG KOH

Carlos, November 30, 2006 (Thu)

A bedroom is not a bedroom unless it has
a means of egress, say the rules for sellers.
After the larks have sung, our Romeo must
have a system for leaving safely and secretly.

It is only after marrying that our lovers find,
at one tragic finish, one another in a tomb.
A bedroom is not a bedroom unless it has
a means of egress, say the rules for buyers.

Outside my room in Queens, a fire escape
for lovers who found their way to my bed.
Staring at its black, complicated extensions,

I wrote my earliest American poems about
freedom and happiness, misery and desire,
the night train frothing on the nearby track.

Andy, April 7, 2007 (Sat)

He would not accept in any part of him,
neither his mouth nor arse, not his ears,
any protruding part belonging to a man,
not the cock, neither finger, toe, nor tongue,

as if, smooth as a pebble washed by the sea,
he was inviolable too, like the seaside stone,
as if to be smooth was to be unbroken
on any and all sides, round as infinity.

But he would allow his whole to be held,
the whole in a part or the part of a whole,
by the hand of a body or the body of a hand,

and taken up by a boyish choice and glee,
aimed with the slant of an eye, and flung –
a planet skipping into the ether of the sea.

Antonio, May 16, 2007 (Wed)

Now 51 and fucking all the boys
on screen and nowhere else, in the half hour
before showering for work, no other time,
sucking in a paunch, straightening the back

when I pass by a mirror or a gorgeous man,
I curse myself for stopping you, Antonio,
from wreaking sweet destruction on my arse,
because neither of us owned a condom.

We took the train for the three-hour ride,
taking in every little station on Long Island,
sensing the ocean when we could not see it,

and just before the train pulled into Montauk
for the weekend binge-eating and sunbathing,
I jumped off – yes, it was just like that.

Andy, June 16, 2007 (Sat)

It's not a design flaw, but a design plus,
the weak digital signal from my phone
to the equally weak receiver in yours,
the call boosted by the tall radio mast,

for our heated talk cannot be stopped
and it cannot stop another's intercourse
as long as we are all on frequencies
slightly different, long undulating waves.

The all-important mast cannot be marriage,
although I'm calling from the home office
in my dear sister's three-bedroom house,

but multiple coordinated arrangements
for long-term care and instant kindness,
in radio cells of the give of honeycomb.

Andy, July 1, 2007 (Sun)

The day after sex should be a day off
for contemplation, walking in the park,
or basically doing nothing at all,
except to reunite the shattered body.

Here comes a leg floating down the river,
the left appendage judging by its toes.
Rescue the right hand, so helpful last night,
before it hunts and gathers yet again.

Now we wait for the torso, the exposed
and powerful chest, the hardworking abs,
the part that's made up of so many parts,

and following behind the skinny ass,
the daily deviser of good and evil,
bobbing like an apple the singing head.

The Editors

Rachael Allen in conversation

RORY WATERMAN

RW: How important is being Cornish to you, and is it important to your poetry? I've read somewhere (though I'd never heard it before) that Kingdomland is an apellation for Cornwall, and the title poem has a Cornish setting, at least implicitly: 'The village is slanted, full of tragedies with slate'. But there doesn't seem to be all that much in the book that is specifically about Cornwall.

RA: This is an interesting question to start! One that I am pleased to answer, as I think somewhere along the line (when writing about my book) a few people got the idea that the word 'Kingdomland' is an alternative name for Cornwall, which it isn't, or at least not to my knowledge. I think someone must have misquoted me at a reading, and I quite like the (very minor) myth-making mistake in its story. Kingdomland is actually a word I found on a very dead forum about Cornwall, where someone had inadvertently created the word 'Kingdomland' by saying something like, 'this is our Kingdomland!', obviously meaning to either say this is our kingdom, or this is our land.

Cornish-ness is important to me in as much as my formative years were there, and my father's side is Cornish as far back as we're able to reach. I didn't realise how special its rurality was, of course, until I'd left. I mean both its sublime beauty and the incredibly unique communities there. They are pirate-y to me in their anarchism. There is something renegade about Cornish people and life that I love, a kind of hardness and no-shit attitude that probably accompanies other coastal communities. The sea-weather gives you good coping mechanisms. I grew up around extraordinarily quick and funny people, who are close to the land, and to animals, and to the elemental parts of a life. When I think about Cornwall I do feel like it's the land health and safety forgot, with kids throwing themselves off quarry walls into lakes and mopeding around moors etc (for fun). There's a relationship with the 'natural' that doesn't seek to romantically objectify, that mines and utilises it as humans are wont to do but not to an extent that resources are drained. I could talk about the poverty, which enshrouds it, but the brilliant, resilient people are what I'm wanting to talk about today.

RW: Do any Cornish poets particularly matter to you? I am thinking of people like Jack Clemo and Charles Causley, who of course wrote a lot about working class lives and specific Cornish settings, often at the same time.

RA: I have to be honest here and say not really. I wasn't really aware of any kind of Cornish scene of writers or thinkers growing up, and now the closest I come tends to be to the visual artists or poets who decamp down there, St Ives poets and painters, or the moneyed surrealists (whose work I adore, but would have had a very different experience to someone like my father, who had a working, farming family). The Cornwall of escaping socialites and the moneyed is not really even Cornwall to me (fair-weather visitors; a January in Cornwall is a very different country to a July), and of Jack Clemo and Charles Causley I know embarrassingly little. I think the closest I come to looking to artists who had a lasting relationship and seemed to understand both the people and the landscape (at least to me) are two who aren't Cornish, but found a home there, the poet W.S. Graham and the painter Karl Weschke. There's a real jaunt in both of these artists' work around the utter bleakness of Cornwall. I think that's what I'm trying to get to here, when I talk about its extremes; it is a dark place with a dark humour, both politically and in terms of how weather-fucked it is, and these two artists processed this in a way that feels very true to its matter. Without sparing us its truth, but also with generative joy.

RW: I nearly mentioned Graham, and I can see some connection. What poets (and other artists) do you think most influenced your own 'formation' as a poet, and how? Where do you think that influence has found its way into Kingdomland*?*

RA: I have many writers I look to for various reasons. I think I'll try and work backwards from those who feel like my most recent obsessions. I don't think I've begun to scratch the surface as to what a poet like Mei-mei Berssenbrugge may give or has given me. The generosity in her poems, to language, to animals, to space, to people, is overwhelming (one of her collections is called *Empathy*, and it strikes me that this word could be indicative of her whole oeuvre). In Berssenbrugge, I see generosity, empathy, curiosity and intrigue all as sites of innovation, which I feel much closer to in regard to how we can 'innovate' in poetry, than in other poetic spaces where 'innovation' can seem posited so adamantly *against* something, that the poems written out of them can lose autonomy or heart. When I read Berssenbrugge I am thinking about how we can be kinder and more empathetic with the world, this is how poems change things, for me. Will Alexander's exuberance, enthusiasm, relentless exteriority mixed with interiority is my poetic bar. These are two poets that mean a huge amount to me. But I actually don't think I write like them at all. Some more writers that directly influenced *Kingdomland*, and my work more generally: Selima Hill, Ariana Reines, Sylvia Legris, Elena Ferrante, Annie Ernaux, Ann Quin, Carolyn Steedman, Carol J. Adams, Kim Hyesoon...

I've just remembered you wanted me to be a bit more specific on my poems and book. This is a terrible trait of mine where I often just hide behind talking about other writers as find it difficult to explicate too much on my own work!

RW: It's okay! We'll get there. How did those writers direct-

ly influence the book? Maybe you'd pick a couple and tell us about those specifically. I hope half of that couple will be Ferrante – that one surprises me a bit.

RA: Ah yes, Ferrante! I think my influence from Ferrante – as much we can / I am able to pinpoint influence and the myriad ways it infiltrates the mind and work, and how that then emerges *in* the work – is probably thematic. Perhaps even that reduces the way I think about her. The way she writes on heartbreak, class, women, gender, violence against women, violence against the self – all kinds of violence really – is something I look to. I also love the way that meaning / story seems to accumulate in her fiction through her very unique sentence structures (and of course, how she has been translated, as I am unable to read the Italian). I feel like she builds worlds slowly, gracefully, with real patience and again, as with Berssenbrugge, a kind of empathy for her characters, even the 'worst' of them. I love how filmic her books are, how cinematic. I don't think I write anything like her but would give all my poems and quite possibly a first-born child to write a book like *Days of Abandonment*, which is my favourite. I would perhaps link the heartbroken, deranged woman at the centre of 'Nights of Poor Sleep' with Ferrante. More Directly, Carol J. Adams and Ariana Reines set a groundwork for how to write about violence against both animals and women, and the industrial complex of the mass violence inherent in animal agriculture. How to be aware of reduction through metaphor, all things I attempted to wrangle with (but perhaps didn't realise at the time) in the book.

RW: I wouldn't regard Kingdomland *as a thematic collection, but the poems are carefully interlinked: it feels as though a lot of work went into deciding on the order of the poems and the trajectory of the book. How important was this to you, and what were you intending to achieve?*

RA: I wrote all of the poems in the book at very different periods in my life – 'Kingdomland' the poem is the oldest in the book. But that poem slightly set the tone (for me) for what I wanted the rest of the book to do, which was to create this quite dark, but fluorescent, carnivalesque kind of world, out of sync but also in sync with reality. I like genre fiction, and I like how genre fiction can give itself shamelessly to the creation of other worlds. I've never felt wedded to representation, which is something I'm trying to work against now, mainly because I always want to work against the things that feel as though they come naturally to me. The shaping of the manuscript came in quite an intense period over about three months before I handed it in to my publisher. When piecing it together, I found new poems emerged. A few of the poems in there were written the summer before the book was published. I'm a big believer in letting a book dictate the poems, not the other way around. I'm not too sure what this means now I'm reading it back, but I'm interested in cohesion in a number of ways, and also meaningmaking through things that aren't necessarily representation, order or chronology (but through sound, image etc). I like the idea of the book as a kind of mesh of meaning or experience that you can read in many ways. A poet I love, Sylvia Legris, does this very well in her books.

RW: You have a habit in some poems of both using and eschewing punctuation – a sort of halfway house some would guard against. Was this habit inspired by any poets in particular? For example, 'Monstrous Horses' begins: 'I jumped I lit the noose / on fire, a great lemon / in place of my heart, a start.' And in 'Volcano', you write 'A bleak a ferrous opening in the sky / a wound the kind that rots to black / rumbling apart, a doctored element of cloud.' I could happily write about what I think you are up to, but I'd rather get your perspective on what you like to do with/without punctuation.

RA: I think I'd rather hear about what you think I'm up to! Quite honestly, I write fast, use punctuation 'incorrectly' and cannot spell (a fantastic start to talking on my work as an editor). I also get my words mixed up, and often find the idiosyncrasies that you note are quite possibly a mixture of a few things. The first is my enjoyment of 'error': sometimes a punctuation discrepancy just feels right for the logic of the poem, but will be objectively 'incorrect'. I'm probably lucky in a way the rules of grammar weren't hot-ironed into my head at school (I don't think I remember ever being taught about the construction of a sentence, or if I was, it didn't stick), or maybe not actually. Another is sound. I like reading my poems aloud and enjoy the reading space. I will often situate punctuation or pauses where they feel right when I'm reading. I also think I look to eschew some kind of syntactical sense when I'm reading, which probably accounts for the quite erratic punctuation. I also feel like punctuation is a good way to aesthetically manipulate a poem. I see punctuation almost as ornament, an interesting thing to make a poem look a certain way.

RW: Since you ask – and I'll keep it brief – I think in some poems your punctuation is primarily rhetorical, the way it is in the work of some playwrights – Sarah Kane, for instance. Elsewhere, of course, you don't use it at all. But in one poem, the untitled piece beginning 'Crying girl', you leave the whole thing unpunctuated but then use a full stop at the end, so each clause flails into the next and yet is a sort of sentence. I think it's effective. What is the 'manipulation' or 'ornament' here, for you? Could you talk about that poem and what you're up to in it?

RA: That poem is part of a sequence that runs through the collection, poems that are indicated in the contents with (I think they're called) 'obliques'. I wrote a number of these very late on in the structuring process of the book. I actually wrote them as structural or architectural pillars of / for the book, and they became the kind of arteries for my thinking in the collection. They gesture to this kind of choral aspect, a kind of group of shadowy girl-figures roaming through and situating. I must admit that my punctuation usage is incredibly... I want to say intuitive (which I think would be generous), but it is probably closer to say 'incorrect'. I write initial drafts of poems fast, punctuation tends to be an after-thought I have to pick at and unspool, reconsidering any of the rapidly plonked commas and semicolons and whatever else I've just thrown in. Not entirely sure what I'm up to, to be honest.

RW: Did Matthew Hollis or Lavinia Singer, your editors at Faber, every try to 'tidy' your intuitions? What sort of editorial input did they have on your book?

RA: They were incredible editors to work with. They are intuitive and thoughtful and taught me a lot about how to approach my own editorial projects. I think the most important thing when editing is to honour a writers' voice, which they did and do so well. Both Matthew and Lavinia helped guide the structure of the book, as well as some important and more specific in-poem line edits (I think we discovered I'd said the word 'blue' an inordinate number of times).

RW: 'Many Bird Roast' is one of your poems I've returned to most, partly because it's at once beguilingly inscrutable and extraordinarily vivid. It's one of several poems in the book implying connections between wealth and meat consumption – in fact, the 'roast' you describe reminds me of Laura Wade's play about the Bullingdon Club, Posh, *which introduced me to the concept of making a sort of fowl Matryoshka. Could you say a bit more about the background to and inspiration for the poem?*

RA: Thank you for your kind words on this! I haven't seen that play, but I'd love to and to read it. 'Many Bird Roast' is one of those poems that seems to fall into your head and onto the page. I don't believe these poems are the product of any kind of muse or luck, but months of reading and work and thinking, which I had been doing before I wrote this poem, around veganism. I have been a vegetarian nearly my whole life, and have been vegan or plant-based for around 6 years. My movement from vegetarianism into veganism was accompanied, as I think it is with many people who shift this way, by intense research and rage around the industrial animal agriculture complex. I am interested in many of the cultures around veganism, and I think was slightly parodying the zealous modern vegan at the kitchen table in this poem (basically, me), the stereotype who pointedly pushes plates of meat away in company: 'I came in, dandy and present', etc. When I was growing up, my family were slightly confused at my vegetarianism, and it was treated almost like an affected eccentricity, an idea slightly above my station. The reality of the situation is that my mum, who worked incredibly long hours at multiple jobs, now had to consider how to cook two dinners instead of one. It taught me at an early age about the political and class implications of food and what we choose to eat. I have struggled my whole life with treating eating and food as leisure, for in my childhood it was presented as sacrifice and struggle. I think these things could all be in the poem.

RW: Your upbringing wasn't much like most London-based editors, I suppose – and of course you're now one of those, at Granta. *I've read about the challenges you felt as a student of working-class parents at Goldsmiths, but do you think that background gives you certain advantages in your job?*

RA: This is a really interesting question, because I have actually never thought about this. Advantages that I can think of are predominantly towards how I can help others. I'm perhaps more aware, or at least, my awareness comes from lived experience, of how hard it can be to access a 'professional' world as someone who is working class, or from a working-class background. I think actually I am not able to answer this question very well, because the truth is I feel like an imposter every single day – and because of the difficulties I have experienced in attempting to be working in the spaces I have wanted to my whole life (writer, editor), I know now that these worlds are just not built for those who are working class. My best friend from home (who also has a professional job) and I were talking recently about our work and his words to me I remember: 'we're not supposed to be here', and it feels true. I used to think the difficulty I experienced was universal; I know now it isn't.

RW: Does publishing have a class problem?

RA: Mainstream publishing has numerous structural issues. In my opinion, its London-centrism is a massive part of this. The easiest way to answer this is, most people in my position – I would go so far as to say everyone else I know – has received or does receive financial support from their parents, or is not or does not anticipate having to support their parents now, or in a not too distant future. This is not the case for me.

RW: What have you tried to bring to Granta *as an editor? What is your ethos?*

RA: I came to my work at Granta after publishing work with my own small press for years, so the ethos of community-based, well designed, almost art-object-adjacent publishing was definitely in the front of my mind as I was working on ideas for the list (and now we have a design that is type-led, with a Risograph feel). Content-wise, it's probably easier to talk about the presses that I love in America which I feel are putting out erudite, unapologetically poetics-led books (that are also fun, funny, moving, bright, essential, etc.), that don't seem to carry the weight of a kind of mannered Britishness I wanted to avoid. I love WAVE books, Ugly Duckling Presse, SoftSkull, Graywolf, Milkweed, Octopus books etc. They put out good & serious poetry untethered, or something. It's hard to articulate, but I wanted to make room for work that experimented, in ways probably outside the British experimental tradition. I wanted to create a home for authors with books maybe unsuited to other lists (perhaps it is more hybrid work), that I felt was not being published otherwise. But really the list moves with the authors, the ethos comes now from them!

RW: Sure, but you choose and have chosen those authors. Could you elaborate on that 'mannered Britishness'? What do you mean, exactly, and what about that makes you want to steer away from it?

RA: Well, now that I'm hearing that said back to me I don't really know. I don't like the idea of value judgements in poetry and I don't ascribe to the idea of sorting writing via it being 'good' or 'bad', or at least, that kind of thinking is not what leads my publishing, and I think the smallness of UK poetry can shove us into these mindsets. Prize-culture (which I hate) dominates because there are very few other outlets for 'validating' people's work and, without scrutiny, it leads easily to hierarchies.

There's a phrase I detest in poetry criticism (that I see a lot in UK reviews), and it's when a poet or a poet's work is deemed 'the real thing'. It makes my skin crawl. The real thing to whom, and in who's canon? Who decides what's 'real', and what does a poem have to be to be 'real'? I think when I say mannered Britishness I probably mean middle-class English strictured-ness, academy-led value judgements and an unquestioning devotion to heritage. I want to work, and be with work, outside these things.

RW: *What's next for you? Are you working on any books or other projects?*

RA: I'm working on a few things, but feel very in the middle of them all! I am trying to write poems as often as possible, and am also – slowly and vaguely, writing a book about class. I'm not sure how this will present itself yet, but I am finding it cathartic to think about the whiplash of class experience in the UK, or especially the experience I have had. I am reading a lot of Annie Ernaux and Didior Eribon, and these writers are helping me a lot.

Three Doorstones

MICHAEL EDWARDS

He thought it paradise with Laura there,
Heaven on earth, the old Romantic! – who
Nevertheless pretended he was wrong:
'Cut off from things... not where I really was.'
Should one believe the vision, or the real
Without the magnetizing glimpse, the fine,
Foolish persuasion of another world?
'How came I here, and when?' His lady's limbs,
Sweet smile, angelic bosom, and the rest
Were his creation for the sake of truth,
The truth that heaven is here and unattained.
His well-read Seneca had said as much,
Or more, of places where gigantic trees,
Grottos whose vaults hold mountains in suspense,
Or sudden waters gushing from the rock,
As at Vaucluse, were signs a god was present.
Old pagan! We know far more facts than you.
You marked appearances we cannot see.
For Petrarch too, the poplar by the spring
That, soaring skyward, shaded river, bank
And all around, was naturally strange,
A place of shadow for the intellect
To think obscurely of the potent earth
Offering living rivers to the air.
Vaucluse was second nature from the first,
A foreign land that maps could not locate,
A countryside, a country, of his own,
A stepping-stone, a threshold, and a door.

*

That clear, and fresh, and soft water that he,
Petrarch recorded and that I, on finger-
Tips and expectant lips corroborated
Once, and so many years ago, in wonder,
Tasting the truth of his exacting numbers.
Heat, Provençal and dry, reigned in Fontaine
De Vaucluse that day and, suddenly, this treat:
A solid peasant-woman, legs apart,
Quietly peeing on the willing ground
In fullest view and unconcerned. In one

Vision the fabled waters and her own.
A telescope of words and I remember
Myself remembering (or someone else)
In a cool and living pool his limpid Tuscan,
His fictive, more than real love, and his
Fortunate exile. Peering at the bubble
Memory, so vivid and so far,
Adrift on the edge of nowhere, of elsewhere,
Other than fact now gathered in my mind
With that strange woman and her streaming wealth,
I seem myself, borne on a skid of now's
Open on all sides, sown in memory,
To contemplate my world as otherwhere,
A precious, coloured globe waiting to be
Shattered and made anew in all good time.

*

The sun's eye followed us from Petrarch's place
To L'Isle-sur-Sorgue nearby and René Char.
A giant standing in the doorway like
A ruined column, then a long handshake,
A careful lifting from a darkened cupboard
Of precious painted barks to exorcize
His sleeplessness, a table stacked with pills.
Our small son crouching on the gravel, Char
Lowered his folding bulk and cautiously
Kneeling at his side, asked what he was at.
'Tu le vois bien, je cherche des fossiles.'
His Tina Jolas, passion, plight and Muse
As he for her, was there, and spoke with warmth.
A caller of two words: 'Maquis Ventoux',
Collecting for survivors and for widows,
Shadowed in the open door the earlier days
Of hero Char's Resistance. Fossils were found!
I bore away a more than handsome gift –
That startling generosity – and saw
His ravaged looks in memory, as now
The sun's glass eye oblivious of all that.
All dead, those elders, and the pages turn.
We meet with death in talismanic night.

Memories of Raymond Williams

DAVID HERMAN

with thanks to Professor Bryan Cheyette

As a student at Cambridge in the late 1970s I attended a number of lecture courses by Raymond Williams on modern tragedy, from Ibsen to Brecht, and on Marxism and Literature. Williams spoke without notes, clearly and concisely.

Two things struck me about these lectures. First, his presence. In the words of his biographer Fred Inglis, Williams was 'unassailably assured', calm, authoritative. His former student Terry Eagleton spoke of 'his deep inward ease of being, the sense of a man somehow centred and rooted and secure in himself.' This was exactly my sense of Williams in the late 1970s.

Then there was his range and erudition. He talked about the history of drama from the Greeks and Racine to Chekhov and Strindberg, about Marxist debates about base, superstructure and hegemony.

Williams was then at the height of his career. During the 1970s he published his Fontana Modern Master on Orwell, a book on television, *Keywords*, *Politics and Letters*, a fascinating book of interviews about his life and work with three key figures from *New Left Review* and one of his best books, *The Country and the City*, which started with the question of how to read the English country-house poems and becomes a powerful social and historical analysis of how writers have idealized the countryside, suppressing the realities of rural labour and property relations.

He was astonishingly prolific. He wrote seven novels and wrote, edited and co-edited almost thirty books of literary and cultural criticism. He was also a regular contributor to the *Guardian*, writing almost three hundred reviews, and from the 1970s wrote a number of long essays for *The London Review of Books* and *The New Left Review*.

Above all, Williams was a key figure in two major shifts in the British Left from the 1950s. First, there was the cultural turn led by Williams, John Berger, EP Thompson, Stuart Hall and EJ Hobsbawm. They were a new generation. Apart from Hall they were all in their Thirties when the New Left began. They didn't just write on politics or Marxist ideas. Berger began writing regularly on art for *The New Statesman* in 1951, Thompson's first major book was on William Morris in 1955, *Culture and Society* in 1958 established Williams as one of the leading literary critics of his generation.

Second, there was the movement towards social history or history from below which changed the way two generations thought about class, society and British history from the English Civil War and the Industrial Revolution to the nineteenth century. In a lecture on Racine, Williams contrasted the use of a chorus in classical drama with the use of *confidents* in neo-classical drama, in particular the relation of masters and mistresses and

their servants. 'There are no citizens in Racine,' he wrote. *The Country and the City* begins with a very moving personal account of his roots in the Welsh countryside, how his father, 'at twelve, went to work as a boy on a farm,' and left 'to be a boy porter on the railway.' The following chapters, among the best Williams wrote, explored how poetry romanticized the realities of life in the countryside. This emphasis on class was one of the most distinctive features of Williams's critical work and was hugely influential during the heyday of the New Left in the 1960s and 70s.

As the critic and historian Stefan Collini later wrote, 'the timing was right' for that whole generation of socialist historians and critics, perhaps especially for Williams. In his review of Fred Inglis's biography, *Raymond Williams*, Collini wrote, 'the early 1960s was *the* time to be a rising star of the intellectual left; certainly, the 1960s and 1970s created a hugely expanded audience in higher education for anyone able to address 'academic' issues in an accessible way.'

It was also the time of the paperback revolution. Many of Williams's best-known books were republished by Penguin and devoured by 6th formers and students flocking to the new universities that were opening up during that time. By 1979, according to the editors of *Politics and Letters*, some 750,000 copies of his books had been sold in the UK, including 160,000 copies of *Culture and Society* alone. *Keywords* sold 50,000 copies in its first two years. It was a time when undergraduates bought books. They had grants and no tuition fees to pay.

Just as important, Williams spoke for a generation of provincial grammar school boys, many the first in their family to go to university. It was a generation born in the late 1920s and 1930s which included writers and playwrights like Willis Hall, Alan Plater, Dennis Potter, Trevor Griffiths, Melvyn Bragg and Barry Hines. He spoke to this working-class generation in a way no other literary critic did.

It was also, crucially, the heyday of literary criticism in Britain. The English Faculty at Cambridge in the late 1970s included Williams, Frank Kermode, Christopher Ricks, Tony Tanner, John Barrell, Stephen Heath, Jeremy Prynne, Tony Spearing and many more. It was a formidable line-up. As Perry Anderson famously wrote in the 1960s, the absence of theories of society in British culture left a vacuum which was filled by literary criticism, first the generation of Eliot, Empson, Richards and Leavis, and then a later generation which emerged in the late 1950s and '60s. It is hard to imagine a literary critic today who could match Williams's standing in British culture but that is partly because the status of literary criticism today has changed so much since his time.

There was something else about Williams's reputation

in Cambridge in the 1970s. He was the leading Marxist critic in the English faculty. At a time of growing radicalism this was an exciting time to be on the Left. The first sentence in *Marxism and Literature* reads, 'This book is written in a time of radical change.' I interviewed Williams in 1978 for *Granta*, then still a student magazine. He was almost sixty, quietly spoken, impassive, his dark hair drawn back, his hands folded. I asked him what he meant by this sentence about 'radical change'. He replied, 'I think that in the late '60s and early '70s, a process of quite structural change in society began, which implied very radical changes inside the Left and inside Marxist theory, so that at every level one had the feeling of entering a new period.'

What I didn't realise then but only discovered later was that Williams was undergoing a dramatic transformation in his own thinking. Beneath the apparently assured surface, Williams was radically reinventing himself during the Seventies and early Eighties. If you look at the books that made his name in the 1950s and '60s, *Culture and Society* (1958) and *The Long Revolution* (1961), they are so English, preoccupied with the Industrial Revolution, the rise of democracy and the growth of literacy. Much of his best writing was about 'the long nineteenth century', from the 1770s and 1780s to the early 20th century. It is full of references to Leavis, George Eliot and Lawrence, Dickens, T.S. Eliot and Orwell.

Leavis and T.S. Eliot, in particular, such influential figures in mid-twentieth-century English culture, cast a long shadow over Williams during his early years as a critic. 'I knew *The Great Tradition* by heart,' he told one interviewer. His breakthrough work, *Culture and Society*, he later said, was inspired by Eliot's *Notes towards the Definition of Culture* and was partly written as a response to Eliot and Leavis. 'The initial impetus [for *Culture and Society*] goes back to '48,' he told the editors of *Politics and Letters* thirty years later,

> when the publication of Eliot's Notes towards the Definition of Culture confirmed something I had already noticed: the concentration of a kind of social thought around this term which hadn't before appeared particularly important. ... Eliot's book quickly acquired great influence.

He wasn't just responding to the dominant figures of his time. Williams often wrote how isolated he was after the war, first at Cambridge and then as an adult education teacher during the Fifties. 'For the next ten years I wrote in nearly complete isolation,' he said. Not just isolated but embattled. His primary motivation in writing *Culture and Society*, he said later, 'was oppositional.' 'I knew perfectly well who I was writing against: Eliot, Leavis and the whole of the cultural conservatism that had formed around them.'

There was also a larger sense of personal crisis. He was 'in a state of fatigue and withdrawal,' he said in later years. In his biography Fred Inglis captures this moment in Williams's life when he left Cambridge just after the war:

> He knew that he wanted to write but not what he could write about; he knew he had a novel in him, but not

that he could write it; he knew he had a marriage but not how to live it; finally, he could sense that his life-project, to urge forward into a more general and generous future the deep, tacit values of his childhood, his father, the flowers, the fruit, the railway, was profoundly at risk in the Britain of 1945, and he feared defeat even as he longed for a victory with a longer future than had occurred to Attlee's Labour Party.

This sense of crisis drew Williams to Ibsen in his final year at Cambridge. Ibsen was already a standard author in the tragedy paper and Williams wrote a 15,000-word dissertation on him which influenced all his later writing on modern drama and became the chapter on Ibsen in *Drama From Ibsen to Eliot* (later *Drama From Ibsen to Brecht*). Ibsen, he later told his interviewers in *Politics and Letters*,

> was the author who spoke nearest to my condition at the time. Hence the particular emphasis I gave to the motif of coming 'to a tight place where you stick fast. There is no going forward or backward.' That was exactly my sensation. The theme of my analysis of Ibsen is that although everybody is defeated in his work, the defeat never cancels the validity of the impulse that moved him; yet that the defeat has occurred is also crucial.

This sense of crisis in the 1940s and '50s passed as he became more successful with the rise of the New Left and the growing popularity of his cultural and literary criticism. A third phase of his career followed in the 1970s when his thinking underwent a further dramatic change. Williams began to engage with continental thinkers like Goldmann and Lukács and with the Marxist tradition. He started to write more theoretical essays on *Base and Superstructure in Marxist Cultural Theory* (1973), *Problems of Materialism* (1978) and *Marxism, Structuralism and Literary Analysis* (1981). He wrote books of essays called *Problems in Materialism and Culture* (1980) and *Writing in Society* (1983), both published by Verso. 'My own long and often internal and solitary debate with what I had known as Marxism now took its place in a serious and extending international inquiry,' he wrote at the beginning of *Marxism and Literature*.

This new more theoretical work attracted younger critics like Edward W. Said. Williams, especially *The Country and the City*, was a major influence on Said's *Culture and Imperialism* (1993) and Said wrote a tribute to Williams for *The Nation* when he died in 1988. Stuart Hall spoke eloquently about Williams in a Channel 4 programme broadcast soon after Williams had died. He analysed a clip from a TV programme in which Williams had talked about the meaning of production. 'In so many different contexts,' Hall said, 'he takes these central words and quietly turns them around so you can't engage with them in the old terms of reference anymore.' In a later piece for *The New Statesman* in 2008, Hall wrote that Williams 'was the most formative intellectual influence on my life.' He went on:

> His books have no comparison among contemporary

writing for range and stubbornness of critical intelligence. In an astonishing variety of modes of writing ... he offered the most sustained critical engagement with the central domains of English cultural life. He not so much engaged the map of English culture as re-drew it.

But in recent years Williams's reputation has waned. Just as he was the right person at the right time at the highpoint of the New Left, he seems out of date today. The early books are curiously insular apart from his work on modern drama but even then, there is little about American playwrights like Arthur Miller and Eugene O'Neill. In *Culture and Society* there is little on the French Revolution, 1848 or the Commune or on Marxism and 19th century European social thinkers. It is as if the English tradition he is discussing is in isolation, cut off from European ideas, as he himself was.

More serious for a younger generation, there is almost nothing on race and empire. In *Politics and Letters* (1979), he is asked about the omission of empire from *Culture and Society*: 'there is only one sentence which alludes in any way to that experience.' Key Black thinkers like Stuart Hall and C.L.R. James are almost entirely absent, though he and Hall co-edited *The May Day Manifesto* in 1967 and knew each other for more than thirty years. There are a few exceptions. In an essay, *Forms of English Fiction in 1848* (republished in *Writing in Society* in 1983) there is a passing reference to two new popular literary forms which included 'the *consciously exotic* [Williams's emphasis], itself often significantly associated with the new epoch of colonization.' He then refers to 'the story of the colonial wars: it is the adventure story extracted from that whole experience.' But that's it.

There are almost no women either. George Eliot is the only woman writer he engages with at length in *Culture and Society*. There's one reference to QD Leavis, none to Mary Wollstonecraft, Jane Austen, the Brontës, Beatrice Webb or Virginia Woolf. In his biography, Inglis speaks of 'the much-noted omission of women from all his writing.' Jane Miller wrote of 'one great silent area' in his thought, women as writers and as critics.

Women and colonialism were not the only major absences in his writing. Cambridge's Professor of Drama barely writes about the great modern gay playwrights. In his best-selling book on *Drama from Ibsen to Brecht* He makes just two references to Tennessee Williams, one to Oscar Wilde, none to Noel Coward, Terence Rattigan or Joe Orton.

He wasn't especially interested in Jewish writers either. There are a few pages on Pinter in *Drama from Ibsen to Brecht* and nothing at all on Wesker. One short chapter on Arthur Miller but no reference to Mamet. The novel was his other great interest, and yet the explosion of Jewish-American writing in the 1950s and '60s, Bellow and Roth, in particular, didn't seem to interest him at all. Nor did the Holocaust. It was just one part of a larger parochialism even though he had helped liberate a small concentration camp on 1 May 1945. It is true that he died before the revival of interest in the Holocaust in the 1990s but did the news not reach Cambridge before? It's worth recalling that his beloved Wales became home to a number of Jewish refugee artists including Martin

Bloch, Josef Herman and Heinz Koppel.

These are startling absences and a new generation of students sees Williams as a Miss Havisham figure, old, remote, frozen in the past. Writing about a new edition of *Politics and Letters* in *The New Statesman* in 2015, Geoff Dyer said that Williams

'is seen as the worthy relic of a vanished, pre-Thatcherite Britain, a socialist writer read by a diminishing audience of Marxists, academics and students. It was the least surprising thing in the world to see, in the Occupy Camp at St Paul's a few years ago, a much-pierced protester reading Berger's *Hold Everything Dear*; it was equally unsurprising that no one was holding Williams's *The Country and the City*.'

This is partly because of three striking failures by Williams during the 1980s. First, and perhaps most surprising, he didn't really engage with Thatcherism. Of course, he supported the Miners' Strike and was appalled by the rise of the Right. But there is no critique comparable to Stuart Hall's writing on Thatcherism in *Marxism Today*, gathered in two books, *The Politics of Thatcherism* (with Martin Jacques, 1983) and *The Hard Road to Renewal: Thatcherism and the Crisis of the Left* (1988) or to EJ Hobsbawm's powerful analysis of the crisis of the Labour Party, *The Forward March of Labour Halted?* (1981). They tried to think through what was happening in Britain in the Eighties, Williams didn't.

Second, apart from an essay on the dissident East German intellectual, Rudolf Bahro, Williams barely engaged with the crisis of Soviet Communism. Perhaps this might have been very different if he hadn't died in 1988, the year before the Fall of the Wall and three years before the fall of the Soviet Union. But *Solidarność* was founded in Poland in 1980, and he didn't write about the great dissident writers and thinkers: Milosz or Shalamov, Pasternak, Brodsky or Grossman. The Cambridge Professor of Drama wasn't interested in Tom Stoppard's plays about Soviet Communism, *Professional Foul* and *Every Good Boy Deserves Favour* (both 1977).

The leading Cambridge political thinker John Dunn wrote that Williams's 'political judgements were often culpably ignorant. His connection with human damage broke off – it was all in Britain – so he had no vision of what had actually happened in the USSR.' That phrase 'human damage' is telling. Williams never acknowledged the scale of the disaster of Stalinism. Those essays on Marxist literary critics don't make up for these larger omissions. What mattered to him instead was the world he grew up in, the world of working-class communities and labour.

Finally, closer to home, Williams didn't really engage with the dramatic changes in literary criticism in the 1970s and '80s. His essay on Lucien Goldmann was published after his death, more than fifteen years after the publication of *Le Dieu Caché*, and George Steiner was writing about Lukács twenty-five years before Williams. His book, *Marxism and Literature* and his lecture on Marxism and Structuralism, *Beyond Cambridge English*, are curiously out of touch. It wasn't really his world. He was formed by a bygone age: Tillyard, who taught him in 1940 and Muriel Bradbrook, whose lectures on Ibsen so influenced him as an undergraduate, Leavis and T.S. Eliot.

In literature, Williams preferred the great realist writers to the modernists. It wasn't just about modernist writers, it was about what mattered to them. In 1987 he gave one of his last major lectures, *When was Modernism?* Inglis describes his analysis of Modernism as 'a ringing rebuttal of its selective ideology of fragmentariness, exile, homeless migration, dislocation.' Instead of exile and migration, he preferred a sense of place and belonging. Stability and continuity mattered to him in ways that fragmentation and dislocation did not.

Much of this had to do with his upbringing in a working-class Welsh community. He was born Raymond Henry Williams in Pandy, near Abergavenny in Gwent, a predominantly farming village, with three or four hundred people. There were two chapels, one Baptist, one Methodist. He was the only child of Henry and Gwen Williams. His father was radicalized by the First World War and was later involved in the General Strike.

The small village was on the Welsh-English border and the border became a dominant image in his life. EP Thompson wrote in his obituary that Williams always lived 'on the border country between the academy and the activist movement.' In his last lecture at Cambridge in 1983, Williams said, 'By my educational history I belong with the literate and the literary. But by inheritance and still by affiliation I belong with an illiterate and relatively illiterate majority.' There was also the border between the novelist and the academic, the insider and the outsider. But perhaps the biggest border of all was between his home town in Wales, a world of farm labourers and railwaymen, and the world he left it for, above all, Cambridge.

He went up to study English at Cambridge in 1939. 'I was wholly unprepared for it. I knew nothing about it,' he told interviewers forty years later. 'The university was totally strange to me when I came off the train.' He said he met 'only one other person from a working-class family at Cambridge.'

Perhaps this is why so many of his best books have two key terms in the title: *Culture and Society*, *The Country and the City*, *Politics and Letters*, *Writing in Society*. It is as if there was always a tension between two different poles in Williams's life. In a tribute to Williams after his death, Terry Eagleton said, 'I think he always knew that there was no way of resolving that tension intellectually.'

'Class, always, is what grips and moves him,' wrote his biographer Fred Inglis. But the problem with class as a central concern, the critic Bryan Cheyette told me in a long conversation, is that it leaves so much else out. He didn't seem to respond to the revolution in British culture in the 1970s and '80s when non-white writers like Rushdie and Kureishi and a new generation of women and gay writers emerged. They just didn't speak to him

and perhaps that is why he doesn't matter to a younger generation today.

Williams was interested in canons and traditions: the English novel from Dickens to Lawrence; modern drama from Ibsen to Brecht, dropping James from Leavis's *Great Tradition* and replacing him with Hardy. But the problem, again, was that he wasn't interested in changing the canon. It's always the same key group of male (and a few female) novelists.

This is perhaps why his books made such popular textbooks. If you wanted to know who were the key English novelists or the great modern dramatists, Williams would have a Penguin paperback which would see you through the course. Many of his best-selling books were based on adult education or Cambridge courses on Tragedy or the Novel.

There is an obvious problem with this. What happens when the curriculum changes? When students want courses (and textbooks) on Rushdie and Maya Angelou not on Hardy and Lawrence, on gay or female playwrights not Ibsen and Strindberg? Williams became less relevant to a generation born after his death.

Stuart Hall and E.J. Hobsbawm were more flexible thinkers. They took on Thatcherism and the decline of Labour, race and colonialism. Even EP Thompson kept on the move: history from below, but then the history of crime and nuclear disarmament. Williams chose not to move on.

Posterity is a cruel judge. Empson, Eliot and Kermode have lasted longer than Williams as critics. Ricks had a bigger range, from Keats and Dylan to Beckett and T.S. Eliot. Ricks didn't think Eliot was antisemitic but unlike Williams he could see that there was a problem that needed to be addressed. Orwell understood Englishness better. Conrad and Naipaul knew more about colonialism.

The gaps and absences in Williams's critical writing loom large. Not just race, colonialism and women. Where is religion in *Culture and Society*? What about ideas of the nation? No Wordsworth or Hazlitt, not much on influential historians like Macaulay and Trevelyan. In his book of essays, *Resources of Hope* (1989), published ten years after Thatcher was elected, she is largely absent.

August saw the centenary of the birth of Raymond Williams. When I think back to those Cambridge lectures more than forty years ago, I wish this would be a moment of celebration and rediscovery. I fear it won't be. His decline is symptomatic of a larger change in the British Left. Identity politics has taken over, in London and a handful of university towns but, crucially, it fails to do what Williams did so well: it cannot speak to a larger audience, accessibly, passionately, and with a lifelong experience of working-class life and communities.

Leda Deflowered

PIERRE DE RONSARD

(Odes 3:20; 1587 version)

a contrapuntal translation by Sam Trainor

non ego fluminei referam mendacia cygni
nec querar in plumis delituisse Iovem
– Ovid, *Heroides* ('Hermione Oriesti') VIII.65–66

First Pose

Love's overwhelming stroke,
holed up in my blood,
has scored your signature –
Cassandra – in my flesh,
the arrow's cut so deep
in cardiac tissue
even the rot of the grave
won't decompose your likeness.

I can soothe the woods
with a chord, when they listen,
but even my own lute strings
won't stem this flow of tears...
the sprinklers can't be cut.
The sun, as it rises and sets,
has never known a grief
so unrelenting.

Your stroppy heart outswells
the mutinies of surf
that drench the Barbary Coast.
You couldn't give a toss
about mine – its jettisoned slave –
my votive offering,
since I was yea-high,
to a stony goddess.

Once Zeus was pricked by love
as hard as this: so hard
he abdicated throne
and thunder-cloud alike.
A vision gripped his heart,
as we're so often gripped,
and drove the regal god
to sample mortal sex.

Quivering with the greed
his randy flame had sparked,
he surrendered godhead
like a sack of plunder.

His scalp, his arms, his flanks
and thorax sprouted feathers:
a plumage whiter than milk
on a carpet of strewn petals.

A chain around his throat
positively breathed
the top-notch workmanship
of hammering Hephaestus.
Its twenty carat links
were mottled with enamel,
gleaming like the colour-arc
of water's skywriting.

The chunky glint of bling
against his downy neck
dazzled like the night's eye
gleaming on fresh snow.
He sculled a rift in the blue,
his wingbeats carving air
with the majestic strokes
of newly feathered oars.

He tore the clouds apart,
the way an eagle swoops
to take a basking viper,
licking at its tender,
newfound youth. He soared
above the swimming hole
where Leda came to wade
and kick back on the bank.

Daylight had filled the skies
above the countryside
when Leda brought her girlfriends
to their usual haunt.
Keen to pick the flowers,
she held a basket painted
with a panorama
of psychedelic colours.

Second Pose

From one end of the basket,
swathed in gilt-edged clouds,
the goddess Eos rises
to spritz the sky with blooms.
Her rippling hair is tousled
by jet streams from the nostrils
of horses, as they dredge
the sun from its sea bed.

Its trajectory curves across
the painted sky to reach
its zenith on the handle.
The horses' sinews bulge
and stiffen with the strain.
They gradually begin
to flag, but stick undaunted
to their uphill slog.

Below, the undulating
waves are so well painted
even an old deckhand
might catch a whiff of sea.
The sun, at twilight, plunges
headlong in the swell
on the far side, sinking down
to the basket's watery belly.

On the brow of a rock face,
a peeping shepherd spots
a wolf, hot-pawing it
towards his cringing flock.
Little does he care;
he's too engrossed in ogling
a snail sliming up a lily,
in the lower meadow.

A marauding satyr,
for a lark, snatches
a hamper and a jug of milk
from another frisky faun,
who bucks and gallops off
to grab his cocky mugger.
Milk gets spilt in the tussle,
all down their beards and their pecs.

Two horny rams butt heads
on either basket end:
the final illustration
on its wicker shell.
This was what she carried –
Leda, cutest of the chicks –
the day an actual bird
would come to womanise her.

One girl's white finger plucked
the tears of fit Narcissus,
and the letters scrawled
in bloody woe by Ajax.

The red carnations blanched
before the pretty pillagers,
and you, Sunshine, you watched
your heliotropes flinch.

The girls had already amassed
a glut of meadow flowers –
buttercups and harebells,
primroses and poppies –
when the unsuspecting virgin
called to her cortège,
'Let's stop picking off
our scented victims, girls.

You're such an upbeat bunch.
I love you all to bits.
Come on! I want to catch
a tune from that sad bird
moping on the bank.'
She ran like greased lightning,
leaving her companions
stranded in her wake.

Leaning over the brink,
she showed the swan her hand.
He shivered with delight
and pecked her limpid knuckles.
Beside her, the cheating fowl
went snaking through the sedge
and gliding suavely on
the surface of the pond.

Then, jaunty as you like,
he arched his wings above
his back and tamed the nymphette
with a serenade.
His stealthy flames licked up
beyond the virgin's knees
and sprayed a bed of blossoms
round about the swan.

At first, he'd seemed so noble,
but now he saw an opening
and snaffled it.
A ripple of his neck
caressed her unfledged breasts,
and then, between her thighs,
he slid his dripping bill
deep in her scarlet mouth.

His bony pinions clamped
her arms. He forced his keel
hard against her torso,
pinning her to the ground.
She squirmed and bit and pinched
beneath the hulking cob,
and yet, amid the struggle,
she felt her girlhood ransacked.

Flecked with madder lake,
the humiliated girl
eventually spoke up.
Her voice dripped with scorn:
'Where did you fly in from,
you feathered freak?
How dare you swan around
molesting princesses?'

'I thought your heart was pure
and white, like its snowy getup.
I know now I've been cursed
by a murkier thing altogether.

I swear to all that's holy,
I wish I was pushing up daisies,
now that my rose has been plucked
in the first flush of spring.'

'I'd rather some widowed tiger
pounced and ate me alive
than this: to be known as the moll
of a random water-bird.'
Her arms and legs went limp.
Her eyes had begun to drown
in the tide of imminent death
as the swan declaimed his reply:

Third Pose

'Babe, I'm not what I appear
to the naked eye;
there's way more grunt beneath
the surface than you'd think.
I'm the King of Heaven,
baby, I'm the guy
who chucks the thunderbolts
against the jagged slopes.'

'Your fleshy pigments glowed
so hot I couldn't help
but slip into this suit
of alabaster feathers.
So quit your griping, girl;
this is your destiny.
From this point on, you'll be
Poseidon's sister-in-law.'

'You'll lay two giant eggs
in which my seed has worked
historic feats of breeding
to shake the mortal realm.
From one, twin boys will hatch:
Pollux, a world-class swordsman,
and his brother, a peerless
dashing cavalier.'

'The other egg contains
a girl so heavenly
her looks alone will raise
an army against Troy.'
She took his speech on faith,
succumbing to her fate,
and, as the words sank in,
she felt her waistband stretch.

This is a controversial theme, to say the least. As far as I know, Ronsard's ode (published in 1550) was the first extended depiction of the rape of Leda by the swan in the poetic canon. Ovid is generally assumed to be the source of the erotic, pseudo-moralistic trope in early modern art, but has only a few stray lines on the affair. The reference in *Metamorphoses* is nothing more than a vignette: a single line describing one of the scenes portrayed on Arachne's titillating moral tapestry. Edmund Spenser, who perhaps knew Ronsard's version, expanded the line into a stanza in Book 3 of *The Faerie Queene*. A superior mention in Ovid is Hermione's eloquent preterition in the *Heroides*, used as the epigraph to my translation. 'I won't recount the lies told by the swan, / Nor say how Jove disguised himself in feathers.'

Ronsard's ekphrastic poem is an ironic unpacking of culturally embedded scenes of sexual violence. It has none of the solemnity of Yeats's sonnet, in which the swan is almost the embodiment of Nietzsche's devil, portrayed by Zarathustra as '*der Geist der Schwere*' (the spirit of gravity). By contrast, H.D.'s 'Leda', published five years earlier, is a lovely bit of languid modernist erotica – perhaps the perfect example of *écriture féminine* – in which the 'red swan', divested of his phallic neck and all divinity, unfurls into a vulvic analogue. It is not a rape at all. In fact the Leda voice transforms the swan into her own '*vermeille bouche*'. In *Three Women*, Sylvia Plath's third voice goes the other way. She says what Ovid's Hermione would not: 'There is a snake in swans... I wasn't ready.' The victim of coercion admits her trauma.

Ronsard's poem is a completely different animal. The sexual encounter itself seems typical of Renaissance male fantasies of irresistible seductive power. But it also parodies them. Even the hammy Petrarchan jeremiad of the preamble is revealed to be tongue in cheek by the ensuing mock-heroic ekphrasis of the painted basket. There are other oddities: the swan wears a heavy collar on a gold chain, ostensibly as a sign of opulence and power, but also a clear index of bondage; the illustrations on the flower basket have a distinctly homoerotic tang, especially the two satyrs wrestling over a jug of milk; and the entire composition appears to revolve around a sniggering literalisation of the euphemism '*défloration*' (deflowering).

A 'contrapuntal' translation is not necessarily antagonistic to its source. Its defining attribute is a playful polyphony: the attempt to create syncopations of rhythm and reference in a simultaneous performance. However, a critical function is an obvious avenue of expansion. This version has one eye on its own unacceptability. It is itself a non-consensual generative encounter. It forces itself, and its contemporary sensibilities, on an 'original' (if that word has any meaning in this context... I prefer the term 'baseline/bass-line') whose subject matter, despite a subtle satire of the glorification of sexual coercion, still undeniably seeks to entertain us with a decorative take on the rape of a young girl.

Five Poems

LUTZ SEILER

Translated by Stefan Tobler

mechanics of the pictorial world

taking down the swing
in autumn & putting it up
in April. day after day

the suburb commutes under
the trees and hour after hour
from the sky above courtyards

pulverised swallows fall & neatly
stuffed ones come up: the
gravity in their eyes hangs

raw as an egg
over the globe over
the man at the next table

(his face he leans in sleep
against the lamp) and over
the slender animals here

that each evening
creep down the promenade
& murmur

ev'nin into the dark as
if tucking the greeting away
in their warm almost

sleeping bodies

fin de siècle

I walked through snow with all the nervous
post-war whip-cracked lamps behind my neck
across Vienna's Mozart bridge and there
a tired Irish setter was still sitting
    tethered he

was dead and waiting for me
as in, I untied his rope
from the railing base and began
to swing the creature a little
to and fro *skin & bony light
the bells are ringing flurry of snow*
    starting I was singing

a little song about the Danube over
and over (I was a child) the dead
setter circled now at the end
of my arm above the lovely
balustrade he curved
light and big into the nervous
post-war lamplight a rip
widened at his throat a whistling

got up and the rigid
skins on his eyes clicked
tiredly open and to: you'd

have loved the mechanics of the gaze
and would have been lonelier still
above the snow, the bridge & the old song

my year, born sixty-three, that

endless succession of children, drilled
into the echo vault of the hallways, creeping
with a stoop into the pocket

of another's, a stranger's coat, seven
    full of wax with a heaviness
inhaled from floorboards, eight

    with a heaviness rising from the urinals'
bowls to our heads, we had
Gagarin but Gagarin

also had us, every morning the same, a scraping
of sleeves over desks in the wake
of writing & every noon
the spoons would strike the hour, we had

table duty, milk duty, the pressure
    of a vacuum in our eyes jelly
    in our ears until
it fell silent
gravity fell silent
    *that was what hurt
    in our caps*

when we peed, in the protective wood
when we spoke, we had
rote slogans: that counter to our planet's shadow sides
 at least *we held up a light*
  first all together & then
   each of us silently
   in private again, we had

no luck. so the houses fall down
  and finally we become
 small once more &

ride back into the villages of wood, of
straw, the ones we came from, cracked & thin
with an echo whetted

on the wind: say hi to Gagarin from us, we
had no luck, we left, back
to our villages
  & the villages' setting forth

over the fields by night...

Greater Berlin, one

The smell of the last allotments & heavy
lifting at the huts: some
 hung sleigh bells on
pockets bulky and hard, late-
returning POWs' greatcoats, we
still had tinsel, rags and tatters in
the cherry trees, bottles, wherever you stepped, on
 the short, brown necks. there

 we perched at the table with splayed-
out partings couple of
pounds of eyes puppies under their lids: lattice
fences, asbestos roofs forever or
a he's-friendly pit bull in the pimps'
 mayhem & crystal-

 clear bottles, first off heavy
and hard to let go, then empty
buried in rats'
 holes, their whistling necks

towards the Western moon. how good
that rat-bashing felt in the
 northwester & what
we here now always have: this

patrolling beyond the tips of the skull, by day
when reverie carefully beds its temples
in layers of air, raw
nerves on bark, on cortex, when

 in early light the head
& life of a bird smack
into each other

but it was good

 to breathe, on
& off went the breath on the bakelite boat
of our lamp, we had
its dark, mechanical light, we had albata
on the ash tray, nails torn
& alone in slates like Crusoe, deep

in the radio slept the radio-child with
 tubes & relays, which it
alone understood, a rattling such
as big ships make, flashing a signal, something
 between off in the evenings, then silent
& quietly on again: alone

 in the dark came
the frequencies later never to be found, local
frequencies of aging, the disappeared
 villages &
their weak chromosome strokes on
 the dials – I

saw Crusoe, my father; he
 went down, baptised, timbers round his temples,
 back home he laughed, the man
with the beaming hand, his hissing, his
 crackling, they hear

how everything ends, slips, *two*
 legs the coastline the soft
 parting of feet in a stride

for Jürgen Becker

Jaccottet and Mahon

CHARLIE LOUTH

The poetry of Philippe Jaccottet, who died on 24 February at the age of 95, having in 2014 been sealed by the 'tombstone', as he felt it to be, of 'entering into' the gilt-and-leather Pléiade, is best-known in English in the translations of Derek Mahon. They were published in Penguin International Poets in 1988, the series in which Mahon's own *Selected Poems* later appeared, and then a decade later in a smaller selection as *Words in the Air* (1998). It's not hard to find affinities between the two poets, as well as other possible reasons which might have attracted Mahon to Jaccottet, however different they also are. In any case, it's a notable and in the end quite rare example of a major poet providing extended versions of a major contemporary without working with someone else or from existing translations.

In his introduction to the Penguin Mahon calls Jaccottet a 'secular mystic' and those words have since been used of Mahon himself by various critics too. Both poets evoke Paul Éluard's idea that another reality exists, but within rather than beyond the world we know. Jaccottet's word for this 'other reality' is 'l'illimité', that which has no limits, and he suggests that beauty arises when 'the limit and that which has no limits become visible at the same time'. Manifestations of such coincidence he looks for above all in the light, in what Mahon calls 'light-readings', and says that poems can be thought of as 'little lamps where the reflection of another light is still burning'. His 'passive attending upon the event', to use T. S. Eliot's phrase, requires a clearing of the ground, a reduction to a state of unknowing, in the spirit of the lines from *Four Quartets* that 'In order to possess what you do not possess / You must go by the way of dispossession' and that 'what you do not know is the only thing you know', 'East Coker' being one of the few English poems Jaccottet includes in his anthology of twentieth-century European poetry. That is the point Jaccottet repeatedly seeks to return to in the hope that it might be a starting-point: 'everything always starts from conditions and uncertainties, from new difficulties. That's also where hope lies: in the dark, in impossibility'. His second collection, *L'Ignorant* (1958), makes a virtue and even a programme of ignorance, and seems to be the collection that means most to Mahon.

For his part, Mahon has spoken of 'the metaphysical unease in which all poetry of lasting value has its source', and what draws him to Jaccottet, and to translate him, may well be that it allows him to entertain possibilities that he can't quite in his own voice except more obliquely. Where Jaccottet is hardly ever ironical, Mahon hardly ever isn't, though his ironies are mostly of the subtlest sort, only just glancing against their subject, rather like the light-effects Mahon's poems are almost as full of as Jaccottet's. There are several places where Mahon seems to be quoting or even parodying Jaccottet, but in a different key, such as the whole of 'The Attic' or this from 'Going Home':

> As if the trees responded
> To my ignorant admiration
> Before dawn when the branches
> Glitter at first light.

Perhaps translation too is always in a sense ironic, refracting its original, both saying and not saying the thing it means, or saying two things at the same time. Certainly it suits Mahon down to the ground, allowing him to be in two places at once, to home in on something distant and make of displacement a kind of home.

Jaccottet first arrives in Mahon's work in *The Snow Party* (1975), thirteen years before the Penguin selection, in the form of a poem from *L'Ignorant*. The poem is called 'Les gitans', and Mahon's translation of it, 'The Gipsies', can be seen as the third part of a triptych of poems about gipsies in Mahon, one in each of his first three full collections. These poems, only one of which is preserved in *Collected Poems*, reflect Mahon's obvious interest in the marginal, in the homeless, provisional and threatened kinds of existence we like to imagine gipsies leading 'on waste / ground beside motorways', as the second poem puts it in *Lives* (1972). And the first two, independent, poems culminate in a too easy, but also admirably candid identification: 'We are all gipsies now', says the first ('Gipsies', in *Night-Crossing* (1968)); and 'the fate you have so long / endured is ours also', says the second (originally called 'Gipsies Revisited'), allowing the gipsies to stand for a general sense of unhousedness, and effecting a characteristic reversal or confusion of the periphery and the centre which despite the irony is fundamentally serious. The third poem, Jaccottet's, also contains a moment in which a 'we' is offered under the sign of ceremonious fragility and exposure – 'âmes de peu de durée' / 'short-lived souls that we are' – but there is a subtler articulation of 'our' relationship to the gipsies, especially in the French:

LES GITANS
à Gérard et Madeleine Palézieux.

Il y a un feu sous les arbres :
on l'entend qui parle bas
à la nation endormie
près des portes de la ville.

Si nous marchons en silence,
âmes de peu de durée
entre les sombres demeures,
c'est de crainte que tu meures,
murmure perpétuel
de la lumière cachée.

The gipsies are the occasion of the poem, but not really its subject. They are probably 'la nation endormie', though the words seem also to enclose the people inside the town, just as 'nous' does not entirely exclude the gipsies camped outside. This helps the poem give us a muted sense of a possible transition, a hope that we may not be quite confined 'entre les sombres demeures'. But the real focus is the audible fire at the beginning, which returns as the 'murmure perpétuel / de la lumière cachée' at the end. Its association with the gipsies lends it a peripheral, perhaps primitive, and occluded quality, and the poem brings us to the brink of either its extinction or, perhaps, its appearance into light. Whereas Mahon, in the poem from *Lives*, addresses the gipsies, this poem addresses the fire, which is a kind of language (it talks and murmurs) and might thus be thought to be telling us something. It is telling us about 'la lumière cachée' which it also is. The poem ends by revealing and concealing this light, which both is and is not the fire we heard about at the beginning. Jaccottet's poem is part of the murmur that sustains and hides it, which is to say that it opens onto or wants to open onto something which for want of a better word we might call mystical or perhaps sacramental. If that is something that can fairly be said to have been entertained more readily in French poetry than in English, that perhaps *enters* more easily into French than into English, especially in 1975, when *The Snow Party* appeared, then bearing this in mind we can have a look to see what Mahon did with it when he appropriated the poem:

The Gipsies

There are fires under the trees.
Low voices speak to the sleeping nations
From the fringes of cities.

If, shortlived souls that we are,
We pass silently
On the dark road tonight,
It is for fear you should die,
Perpetual murmur
Around the hidden light.

Like the original, Mahon's poem ends on 'hidden light', but because the murmur does not voice it but surrounds it, it doesn't quite have the reach and charge of the French. 'murmure perpétuel / de la lumière cachée' hinges between the sound of the fire and something stranger and more urgent that persists at the edge of our world, whereas Mahon seems to domesticate the light by making it a centre and by connecting it much more exclusively with the camp fire. This proceeds from his rendering of the opening lines, where instead of having the fire speak softly ('on l'entend qui parle bas') he seems to make the gipsies speak, so that the perpetual murmur is of voices 'around' a fire. In the later manifestations, in the Penguin Jaccottet and in *Words in the Air*, the beginning is tinkered with, but the misreading or adaptation persists despite an improvement to the 'sleeping nations', so that the mystical element represented by the light is toned down in favour of Mahon's

interest in the gipsies themselves, who in Jaccottet's poem are never really anything more than a starting-point. Despite this shift of emphasis, Mahon's poem still allows a glimpse of something mysterious at the end, and without the playfulness and distancing to be found in the poem which in *The Snow Party* came immediately before 'The Gipsies', 'The Mute Phenomena', again a translation, which has the line, some way after Nerval, 'God is alive and lives under a stone'.

Mahon reprinted 'The Gipsies' in *Poems 1962-1978* without change, apart from to typography, in a group called 'Three Poems after Jaccottet'. It was joined by 'The Voice' and 'Ignorance' but later, in *Adaptations* (2006), replaced by 'Words in the Air'. Like 'Les gitans', these poems, 'La voix', 'L'ignorant' and 'Paroles dans l'air', all come from the collection *L'Ignorant*. They are singled out in Mahon's work by being collected in different contexts, apart from the other Jaccottet versions. This is 'La voix':

Qui chante là quand toute voix se tait? Qui chante
avec cette voix sourde et pure un si beau chant?
Serait-ce hors de la ville, à Robinson, dans un
jardin couvert de neige? Ou est-ce là tout près,
quelqu'un qui ne se doutait pas qu'on l'écoutât?
Ne soyons pas impatients de le savoir
puisque le jour n'est pas autrement précédé
par l'invisible oiseau. Mais faisons seulement
silence. Une voix monte, et comme un vent de mars
aux bois vieillis porte leur force, elle nous vient
sans larmes, souriant plutôt devant la mort.
Qui chantait là quand notre lampe s'est éteinte?
Nul ne le sait. Mais seul peut entendre le coeur
qui ne cherche la possession ni la victoire.

And this is 'The Voice':

What is it that sings when the other voices are silent?
Whose is that pure, deaf voice, that sibilant song?
Is it down the road on a snow-covered lawn
or close at hand, unaware of an audience?
This is the mysterious first bird of dawn.
Do you hear the voice increase in volume
and, as a March wind quickens a creaking tree,
sing mildly to us without fear,
content in the fact of death? Do you hear?
What does it sing in the grey dawn? Nobody knows;
but the voice is audible only to those
whose hearts seek neither possession nor victory.

Despite the fidelity of its beginning, Mahon's translation is clearly setting out to make a discrete poem, perhaps a poem in dialogue with its original more than a servant to it, though it wavers between the closeness of beginning and end and the independence most obvious in the dropping of the place name Robinson and the introduction of rhyme. But more significant is the treatment of the mysterious voice itself, which forfeits some of its mystery as it comes across into English. 'This is the mysterious first bird of dawn', Mahon says, disregarding the cautioning of the French: 'Ne soyons pas impatients de le savoir / puisque le jour n'est pas autrement précédé / par l'invisible oiseau'. The original doesn't actually equate the voice of the title with a bird's voice, and simply implies that it is *like* a bird's whistling at dawn. It may be a bird's song, but the French allows for the possibility that it is some other voice, just audible, but not knowable. What then modulates into an assertion – 'Une voix monte [...] elle nous vient / sans larmes, souriant plutôt devant la mort' – is in English slightly weakened by becoming a question: 'Do you hear the voice increase in volume / and [...] sing mildly to us without fear, / content in the fact of death? Do you hear?' It is not exactly a sceptical question, but the difference in tone is just enough to allow the possibility of doubt. The poem's last question is also differently inflected in French and English: 'Qui chantait là...' becomes 'What does it sing...'. The French question is about what sort of presence we are dealing with, whereas the English,

by the end, takes that presence for granted, having translated it into the real voice of a bird.

There is a similar distancing perhaps in 'Paroles dans l'air' / 'Words in the Air'. In the lines 'vous lui disiez que la lumière de la terre / était trop pure pour ne pas avoir un sens / qui échappât de quelque manière à la mort', 'avoir un sens' could have been translated as 'have a meaning', but by going instead for 'point a direction' Mahon again detaches himself a little, a bit like in 'The Gipsies': the light does not itself have a 'sens' but 'somehow' points to one. Though Mahon is certainly drawn to the kind of openings onto a potential 'reality in this' that Jaccottet is after in his poems, there is a guardedness too, and the ironic break of translation is not quite enough on its own to accommodate the difference in what they are willing to credit.

MENARD PRESS

Augustus Young

The Credit: A Comedy of Empeiria in Three Acts
£9.99

Light Years: A Memoir
£14.99

M.emoire (prose and verse about his wife Margaret)
£9.99

Dánta Gradha (Early Irish love poems)
£9.99

Lampion and his Bandits (Literature of the Cordel in Brazil)
£6.99

Days and Nights in Hendon (sequence of poems)
£4.99

Inpress Books: enquiries@inpressbooks.co.uk
Menard Press: pierremenard@menardpress.co.uk

from *Book of Days*

PHOEBE POWER

The following is an extract from Book of Days, a long poem recounting a journey along the pilgrimage route to Santiago de Compostela in northern Spain. This extract describes the ninth and tenth days of the walk, from the town of Los Arcos to Torres del Río, and on to Logroño.

•

9.

We wait an hour in the plaza till it's unlocked, then
pilgrims pour in, extensive gold vision of riches,
rrretablo.

    Seated in the centre
    the little (black) virgin with blue eyes
    from C13th and modelled
    from the island of France
    where they have a lot of black virgins.

    In 1947 they *restored*
    her and *removed*
    her black colour. Smooth black hair
    and tight, smiling eyes,
    her cheeks all powdered.

        Meanwhile, painted faces scream
        their letterbox mouths, cross-eyed
        on the trompe-oeil organ

        The retablo generally
        cold, spiky: solidified
        gold going to break off in bits

Every few metres,
stop to adjust the straps. Pick up.
    stop to drink. Go on.
    Sit down. Sven and Cecilia
coming through trees, don't see me.
Unlace, toe joints
click and stretch soft pink, dry
and hardening. Wrap
again in new soft socks; resume.

*

    Jin-young and Jin-young arrived earlier on; now
they're cutting bread and tomato at a table set in the
doorway.
    I shower, bring my things and notebook down to be
with them. The younger, quieter in English, lets the

other do the talking:
    We haven't found any young men on the Camino!
They're too fast; the women go behind with the old
people
    We're going to cook Korean food at the next
albergue. We'll find – what's the word? Sharekitchen.
We're gonna cook noodles. You can have with us!

I lead us to the tiny church, twinkling a few metres
from our seats.

    swept-up arches,
    faces in the corbels:

    wind   ears
    man   cat
        fish
          mouth

    a tight arch-knot
    roof, islamic star
    and circle at its navel

    and the chequer relief
    outward, flickering squares.

The other girls have left. The site attendant
chatters in Spanish, louder than the building.
There is no
consecration, no
permission to bathe here

*

At dinner I feel
sick and have to leave abruptly

blue, & orange, gold
& the gold coming down,
filling up the red
 leaves

and matching my geranium
shirt, ocean-
 blue shorts

 people still try
to take pictures of the sun,
clicking along with their sticks

...and I think about Stainton C. of E. Primary School, the hymn books that were so surprising to me, their soft covers printed in blue (Book 1) or green (Book 2), titles printed with a chalk effect and drawings of laughing children with bowl-cuts. They soon got a new, plainer set with glossy covers, and by the time I left the school we were singing along to CDs. When I was six I found it hard to read the words at the same time as singing them; I didn't know the tunes and I sang the word 'chorus'.

In assembly we put our palms together to pray and I watched the skin on my wrists wrinkle up in folds. We peeped as our headteacher Mr Shelton closed his eyes, and could not see us. We eyed him in his resolute quietness as he spoke on our behalf: we watched him in his weakness; he was at our mercy

 and hearing the grace the first time, Mrs Grant's abrasive FOR WHAT WE ARE ABOUT TO RECEIVE and the children bang their lunchboxes bawl MAY THE LORD MAKE US TRULY THANKFUL then pop their cheesy Wotsits. I didn't understand the incantation, its strange grammar and call and response. It was the same the first time I participated in Evensong and the psalms were sung with breaths in certain places according to the commas, and I didn't know the words of the creed or the confession which were not printed anywhere.

Recorded singing
adds to the dead feel

 old retablos
 hanging off the walls

all the saints are strong
 white knights with polished heads

 virgin de nieva with a crisp silver head

*

John from Hull joins us for dinner: he's compact and muscular, doing it all in 14 days with a tent.

Why? we wonder. Well I'm a fit lad, and wanted more of a challenge.

Philip arrives sorry I've been at Mass. He works in Dublin with ex-offenders. Have you met the jailors? Ah! No, but I'd know them.

There's not enough room for everyone's plate, wine, water and bread: John's water tips over the paper placemat. I'm a born-again Christian, he's saying, faith, that's why I'm really doing it, I should have said that before.

He scrambles from the table, skipping dessert, and sets off in the dark again. He'll camp on the path, between towns, wherever he happens to land.

Well I couldn't do that, as a woman, says Caroline. I came because I wanted to prove to myself that I could, now that I'm sixty. My father used to take us in the car and just drive, he had that adventuring spirit. My mum still worries but I always had that spark of adventure in me.

Philip's plate of fish peers over the edge of the table and tips up on to the floor. No dinner for a hungry pilgrim? But the kitchen whips up another – flash-fried, Philip says, and it's fresher, more delicious than the first.

At the Sea Wall

HILARY DAVIES

Dawn unwraps the town –
Dun-grey, slate-grey, pale oyster-light;
In the air, like a veil, fine rain.
Mussels and whelks tick
As the tide turns around;
They must weather out the tender time
When the wrack hangs on the harbour stair,
When the nets are picked over.
It's vertiginous down to the bilge and plastic bottles
Scumming the sluices; clam-cold
The planks are stacked like bones.
A saw screeches in the repair sheds,
Paint and turpentine and ooze salt
Everywhere here under the fog's tarpaulin.
You can hardly see beyond your hand,
Not even the promontory light
Nor the lifeboat station.
Out of sight, the sea rocks like a whale sleeping.

*

Gently the traveller comes along the quay,
Stepping with care amongst the ropes and chains.

> Will the boats run
> In the great fog?

The horn is sounding far out across the bay
And the hour, too, from the island,
Calling and warning, sisters.
The tongue in the harbour chapel trembles
Remembering the journeys –
Foodstuffs, clothing, remedies,
Never knowing rightly for how many –
As they came and came
Down the hill onto the grey shore
And got the tough blessing of the ferryman
Shouting and trying to sort them.

> Will the boats run
> In the great fog?

> In the bleak oyster-light,
> On the desert sea?

The lifeboat has slithered down the slipway
And is circling on invisible patrol.

*

> The sea, the sea
> Each man dreamt it
> On the wherries
> Long ago

> The wash against the keel
> At dead of night
> Stars' swell
> And compass light

> Ocean's rising ever falls
> Down the purple deep
> In the skeltering gale
> Terror and truth meet

> Sailors' entreaty
> The rigging's cry
> No unbelievers
> On the sea's vast eye.

*

Gently the traveller comes along the quay:
Andrew and Peter Morgan,
Boatbuilders by the harbour wall,
Have a fine smack almost ready.
They're smoking and cracking jokes;
Maybe their wives will come down later.
But this newcomer wants passage –
He has been asked to go to the island –
They can all hear the bell.
He sits on the wall, scraping shapes in the dust
While they discuss him.
Lack of wind's not the problem
With an engine, and radar,
In theory, lifts the fog's veil.
Yet why, in this weather?
Why risk the channels
As they suddenly change,
And everyone knows
The unexpected always arrives?
Beyond the jetty
Fishermen clatter their lobsterpots.
A lathe turns, somewhere.

Then silence. Even the seagulls are silent.
A breath, a look, a cigarette butt in the water.
The moment's abundance.
Carefully, the traveller descends the sea ladder
And they wrap him in their coats.
The normal bustle, untyings and stashings of things
Ready for the harbourmaster's light.
It is time. The bell sounds continuously
Out of the cloud. It is time.

*

Round the sea wall, the boat dips into her channels,
Grey upon the swell, and tilting slightly
As the world shifts to the weight of her cargo,
That faint breath from her prow,
A whisper lighting the sailors' hair.
In readiness, the island gathers up her multitudes,
The sheep in the heather lift their heads,
The children in the schoolyard hesitate,
The wracked trees lean towards the water:

Is it true?
Out of the stillness the sound of voices
Glances as a note off glass,
Ringing beneath the surface.
A finger ripples along the shore
And the sea's grain flickers
Like mackerel rising
To array the boat
With all her shining outriders
Inquisitive for the upper air.

There is a story to tell, a tell-tale

Anthony Barnett at Eighty

CAROLINE CLARK

Anthony Barnett and I have been friends for almost eight years – since I moved back to my hometown of Lewes, where he has been living for some forty years. I wonder whether our paths would ever have crossed if it hadn't been for an email from David Caddy asking whether I knew about a new journal called *Snow lit rev* issuing from this town. I immediately wrote to Anthony telling him about myself, in part how I had a special interest in Celan and Mandelstam, not knowing he had translated poems of theirs. Within twenty-four hours he had brought to my house on Mount Place, from his place on Mount Street, copies of his 300-plus page volume of translations and 600-plus page volume of poetry and the first issue of *Snow lit rev.*

I was peculiarly prepared for our first meeting a few days later: I had avoided 'doing' English literature at university having studied German and Russian and then Modern European Literature; I had spent all my twenties in Moscow, where I had imbibed a distinctly non-industry idea of the poet. In fact, I had got quite a culture shock moving back West, to Montreal, where writing was suddenly a career once again. And so I could most certainly 'relate' to this poet who felt out of place in the English cultural landscape and who was scathing of most directions UK publishing had taken.

Anthony Barnett is a poet, translator, essayist, publisher, typesetter, percussionist and historian of jazz violin. For this piece celebrating him at eighty I have written to those who know him and his work. I not only include, but am very grateful for, their responses, which shine much-needed light on his work.

Born in a blackout on 10th September 1941, he grew up in the suburbs of London. He worked in business for seven years, towards the end of which he moonlighted at Better Books off Charing Cross Road. He became fully employed both there and earlier at Zwemmers. In 1969 he moved to Denmark as a percussionist with John Tchi-

cai and then Norway. During this time an early book, *Poem About Music*, was published by Rosmarie and Keith Waldrop's Burning Deck press. Two years later, in 1975, he published *Blood Flow*. I'll quote here from Peter Riley's review covering the 2012 publication of *Poems & and Translations* and that is available to read on *The Fortnightly Review* site: '*Blood Flow* established his poetry because the sequence made sense of the modernistic, fragmented, writing he was already doing. The sense of occulted narrative made it possible for the small poems to echo and reverberate against each other within a conceptual theatre, and to offer the reader paths through the scattered instants.'

The review is indispensable to anyone wanting a deeper sense of the evolution of Anthony's writing, but this description of an 'occulted narrative' in itself gives great insight into how the poems function: there is a sense of a story, drama, but stripped of autobiographical detail. The lack of the paraphrasable element – an aboutness – paired with an intense sense of drama characterises, in particular, the earlier work. This lack of an aboutness will always be found 'difficult', 'impenetrable', and even 'hermetic' by some. But perhaps the reader can let go of this craving for familiar fixtures and furnishings and go with the exploratory movement of language. Tony Frazer at Shearsman has commented that 'Anthony Barnett is like no other poet of his generation, yet both his elliptical lyrics and his work in longer spans should be part of the current consensus of what constitutes our modern poetry.'

Returning to England in 1976 he studied for an MA in Theory and Practice of Literary Translation at the University of Essex. For his dissertation he translated the poems of the Norwegian writer Tarjei Vesaas. One might think, as I used to, that the ability to speak and read a language fluently is a prerequisite to translating it. Indeed, Anthony does know Norwegian very well, but he has also translated poems from French (Supervielle, Giroux, Albiach, for example), German, Italian (Zanzotto in particular), Japanese, Russian and Swedish (Lagerkvist, Ekelöf, an essay by Dagerman). He does not speak all these languages; he sometimes works with the help of collaborators and literal translations, but the final poem is his work. His translation of Mandelstam's long poem 'Nashedshii podkovu', 'Whoever Has Found a Horseshoe' (originally published in PNR in 1989 and recently up-dated in *Long Poem Magazine*), is, I had to admit, the best I've seen.

Along with his translations, Anthony also published under his Allardyce, Barnett imprint the first collected editions of J.H. Prynne, Douglas Oliver, Andrew Crozier, and Veronica Forrest-Thomson: publications which emphasised '[t]he enormous part played by Barnett in the promotion of both British and European poetry...' (from Ian Brinton's account on the Anthony Barnett archive held by Cambridge University Library).

From around the publication of *Carp & Rubato* with Invisible Books in 1995, his books often contain sections of longer line poems and sections of prose. His most recent book published this year is titled *Book Paradise: Spillikins*. Spillikins? You know – the game where you drop a handful of sticks and take turns picking them up one by one, trying not to disturb the others. With beautiful illustrations by Lucy Rose Cunningham, and a portrait photo by Sung Hee Jin (both of whom are contributors to *Snow lit rev*), the book is made of the lines that he has picked up, often with a sense of wonderment, along the way. With epigraphs from Gertrud Kolmar and Nelly Sachs and an end quote from Giuseppe Ungaretti – all of which speak of an inability to write, the lost word or words coming to an end – this book is written in now prose passages, now shorter lines of poetry. The prose lines speak of a sense of failure, inability, everydayness: 'My blank thoughts work as a distraction. Worries. Quite enough. They don't have to work particularly hard. /.../ There is still a story to tell, a tell-tale. Give me a break. You and your stories. I'm off for a walk in the wooded countryside.' They stop and start, self-interrupt and peter out. The poem lines are free, surprising in their flight: 'He does not die he sings / To hell with the subscript / Define and defy your beauty / You. You are picking up pieces. / If I am happy to have written one word. / Then, the end of a page. / Like a children's game.' This prose-failure vs. poetry-freedom dichotomy is of course not clearcut. Things fall where they fall.

Anthony Barnett is a poet who over his six decades of publishing has said to hell with a lot of things. To hell with the taboo of publishing your own work. Being a master typesetter and maker of books he knows what he wants from a book, and often he is the only one who can do that in terms of typesetting and production, as evidenced in the *Snow lit rev* journal he and Ian Brinton edit.

Make no mistake, Anthony Barnett is the rarest of things: an English poet who is truly European and of the greater world. In sensibility he walks a kind of poetic *via negativa*: moving always against, resisting. Mandelstam, in his most dazzling of essays titled 'Conversation on Dante', describes the movement of a boat tacking against a headwind. In order to get somewhere there must be this movement against: the poetic word incorporates a movement towards concurrently with one against. This is the tack of Anthony Barnett's poems; they are set in motion towards-against. If there were a dative case in the English language, it could be born here in this unrelenting resistance which gives us movement, exploration and engagement.

*

It's almost an impossible task to sum Anthony up as he's made many interventions across many different fields. But in each field that I'm aware of – poetry, translation, publishing, music – he has remained committed to opening up these fields not only to new insights but also to new voices and perspectives from which so many have learned and benefitted. He should be a cultural institution, but perhaps, more significantly, he remains a man on the wire without trajectory, destination or arrival. At least, that's how I continue to think of him.

DAVID MARRIOTT

Anthony Barnett is a one-off poet and a singular individual. He is ultra-obsessional, but that is a neutral term or perhaps compliment in my book, and in any case goes with the territory, if you look at his achievements as writer, publisher and polemicist. He is to be cherished for his manifold contributions to poetry, poetics and music. His freedom has been difficult and hard-won, but the impression is that he is free at last (to quote an American hero), which is a blessing.

ANTHONY RUDOLF

From his very first book, Anthony Barnett's world has been his own. A world, that is, of the mastery of a language. His eye and ear straightaway knew the exact weight of each syllable – as exact as it was deeply moving. He has never ceased to work this form and to define the present of the poem. Works like this are rare. (For example, to mention a few names: Celan, Oppen, Prynne.) They carry us and they take us into the veritable tearing of the act of writing.

CLAUDE ROYET-JOURNOUD

Anthony Barnett's work is indebted to some yet beholden to none – a rare occurrence on any literary scene, and an important window onto his writing, translations, and research. His latest collection, *Book Paradise: Spillikins*, hints at this. Playfulness, if well-designed, will not be patterned after anything but chance, the child of distraction and thoughtfulness. Thus inventiveness feeds into, not on, curiosity. Perhaps the secret to being the most youthful poet at only 80.

XAVIER KALCK

My contacts with Anthony mainly concern music research. What I would like to point out is how helpful he is as a colleague. In my case this goes beyond discussing matters and sharing information. For far more than a decade now Anthony has proof-read dozens of my articles, often about matters which may be of little interest to him, in order to help me avoid language mistakes. It is a favour that I cannot return, even if we sometimes discuss subtleties in pieces of German literature, and he provides it not only with his enormous knowledge of language matters but also as if it were a pleasure. Few people are so kind.

KONRAD NOWAKOWSKI

Anthony's poems and translations don't repeat themselves formally or prosodically. He has a tactful ear and an always intelligent instinct for – in translation – mimetic solutions that correspond without replicating the pulses in the original poems. His own poems are likewise sure-footed and unexpected. He is a superb book designer and typographer, consummately contemporary because so deeply rooted in the best elements in the traditions he has chosen for nurture. He also has a 'manifest integrity' in the sense that he prefers to out foolishness rather than ignore it. I have benefited from this forthrightness. I believe he knows how good he is: very. Very.

MICHAEL SCHMIDT

I just fished out *Fear and Misadventure/ Mud Settles*. It reminds me of those days. It's signed May 1977. We lived in a small black wooden clapboard cottage then on the Essex Marshes. Anthony had most probably driven over to give us the book. Sometimes he'd visit with Douglas Oliver who lived nearby. Other times he'd just turn up to have a chat, spend time and have a meal. He was studying at Essex at the time and we'd bump into each other on campus. Our conversations always touched on poetry and it would circulate through our lives. Through the years we've kept in touch through his books and publications. Sadly, we've only met up a few times since but Anthony was always as he was easy going, witty, mischievous and warm, and, of course, serious about poetry.

RALPH HAWKINS

I've known Anthony and his work now for just on 53 years. My first pamphlet publication was shared with him and Nick Totton. I can't imagine poetry without his exact and exacting presence, his doggedness, his unexpectedness, his rejection of untruth, and the austere light and beauty of his writing.

IAN PATTERSON

Anthony knows more about jazz violin than anyone else on earth, not just about the music but about its creators, and we are blessed that he shares it so generously and eloquently. He also makes music, as a unique percussionist, and with words. The title of his latest gem, *Fallen from the Moon*, refers to its subject, the hitherto totally obscure Juice Wilson, but it also fits its truly unique author.

DAN MORGENSTERN

Anthony was the first to publish my work, and he's always been so generous to me. I met him at a poetry magazine fair in 2017. I was drawn to his table, the very uncluttered, simple & elegant covers (and to his Snow sweets!). And then his book *Lithos* caught my eye – 'Lithos' being 'stone' in Greek – and I asked him about it. It turns out that the Greek meaning was and wasn't the meaning of his *Lithos*. Over time I learned that this seems to be true for how Anthony approaches language and the humour he finds in it. Always some hidden little puns or layers.

CALLIOPE MICHAIL

I've known Anthony since I was 15, when we met at poetry readings in Dulwich. As our lives have criss-crossed each other in the 57 years since, he has always supported my work, sometimes in very significant ways, and I have endeavoured to support him as well. His energy to make things happen, in poetry, music and other art forms, seems inexhaustible.

NICK TOTTON

I would like to say how pleased I am that *PN Review* are celebrating Anthony's enormous and unique contribution to poetry.

FIONA ALLARDYCE

The Atlas upon whose mighty shoulders sits the earth-sized life and times of Stuff Smith . . . and Ray Perry and Eddie South. . . . We are grateful to our own Saint Antonio, bravo il mio genio.

With admiration, your pal, DAVE SOLDIER

Blood Flow and *A marriage* have such a hesitancy about them, they're so charged, like the interior is shelled out and furtive, but alive. *Poem About Music* is I still think absolutely genius, so self-effacing, so generous, so rigorous. It feels really peerless. I feel like the conditions of its composition depend on Anthony's concept that improvisation = music & poetry = composition, and that the two worlds can't meet. But then from that (quite austere) delimiting, this joyous, really volatile, but controlled text emerges. It's one of the only poems I can think of that feels fully justified.

JOSEPH PERSAD

We crossed paths thanks to his wonderful translation of Des Forêts' *Poems of Samuel Wood*. I do not know any other publisher, poet and translator as genially critical and perfectionist as he is. I am really glad that he's part of my life, not only because of his knowledge, also because he has become a very good friend.

BIBIANA MAS

AB's English is always alive to other languages, partly translating such echoes through itself. I published his translation of Alain Delahaye (*The Lost One*) which also has an AB illustration, and I regard him as the finest English translator of Zanzotto. More broadly, he is able to transmit music from one texture to another through the paradoxes and ambiguities essential to any particular language which he is so sensitive to. In those terms, *Snow* represents an eventful literary assemblage with its visually fascinating musical scores, art-work and photographs threading their way through poets either in translation or working with an array of variant Englishes, sometimes as a second language.

PETER LARKIN

Happy Birthday, Anthony, a cherished poet and prose writer who never procrastinates, your translations robe ineffable truths.

NAOKO TORAIWA

Anthony Barnett is a man of unconditional hospitality. It dictates his total commitment to friendship beyond language barriers and cultural boundaries, as much as his direct (i.e. never behind their back) attacks on his foes including those who relinquish communication. It also commands his forensic search in his music research and never-ending pursuit of musicality, image and le mot juste in his poetry. What is clear, as all his friends know, is his unparalleled sincerity. He always 'approaches' you, with genuine curiosity and compassion, to be with you.

KUMIKO KIUCHI

It is too easy to equate Anthony's poetry with the snowy aesthetic of the volumes in which it has been issued. His more recent writing is poised between serenity and disquiet: the apparently sheer surface of a text proves to be riven with disconcerting fissures, while an extended meditation is contained within the intricately hollowed substance of what seems at first glance to be a casual daybook entry.

PAUL HOLMAN

I first came across Anthony Barnett's poetry properly while reviewing regularly for *PN Review* many years ago. I had been sent, along with a number of other books of poetry, the sequence, or constellation, of about forty brief poems, none more than eight lines long, entitled *Little Stars and Straw Breasts*. It was quite unlike anything I had come across before – in its improvisatory form, its subtle eroticism, and its anguish; in the way brief, surprising lines as well as cunningly juxtaposed words struck sparks off each other; and in the acute sensitivity to the qualities of vowels and consonants that it displayed.

TIMOTHY HARRIS

There are people one admires for a single kind of accomplishment, others whose contributions cross boundaries among fields that are intimately related but have been artificially separated. Anthony Barnett reminds us that the poet's responsibility to the work extends to its publication. His books' unfailing elegance and lucidity in appearance make a promise that his writing fulfils. Too many poets seem indifferent to the physical and visual dimension of their publications. Anthony's work is a reproach to such laxity.

BARRY SCHWABSKY

As poet and publisher for the past fifty years Anthony Barnett has ploughed a solitary furrow, unerringly straight and hauntingly evocative across the field of English poetry. That furrow owes little to a notion of landscape or cityscape as it is conceived within the confines of much British poetry over the last half-century and as both editor and poet he has always stood on the side of the island which faces the Continent. His sense of clarity and space was what prompted J.H. Prynne to assert that 'You have the word lodged in the ear's labyrinth like a little pebble within that delicate fluid, otolith which sways to the sound passing over it.'

IAN BRINTON

I like to think of Anthony Barnett as a collector of strays. I think he has an uncanny ability to recognize something stray-like in the artists and works and memories (and typefaces, for that matter) he discovers and assembles. As a consequence, every time an issue of *Snow* comes out, it's as though we've all been invited to a multinational dinner party of strays, tenderly orchestrated by a host (who finds meaning in even the seating plan) whose talent to collect is matched only by his generosity to give.

SHEREE CHEN

Poems

TRISTRAM FANE SAUNDERS

Crystal Palace Park

I. The Head

In the middle of a lockdown, I am lost
in the living maze. The hornbeam hedge, unminded
now for months, remembering its lopped

limbs, grew headstrong, wildering, it blinded
its own eye, sewed shut the famous rings,
turning against the maker that designed it.

Turning again, each path re-roots to bring
me – though I hardly mind – to the same dead
end. I have forgotten everything

but these three things: the root of *Penge*; the head
-less sculpture loitering outside the maze;
and one more piece of what I'd always said

was useless *trivia*, which means three ways,
a forking road, the point where lost begins.
Lost in the mid-Eighties, it was Dante's,

the head. I'd like to think it wore a grin.
Penceat: from the Welsh for 'head' and 'wood'.
Whichever way I turn leads further in.

The statue's standing where Penge Place once stood,
demolished for that looking-glass, the Palace,
whose weightless walls shine like they never could

when it existed. Living backwards, Alice,
has one advantage in it, said the Queen.
I don't remember it. Pre-emptive malice?

Or knowing that we're where we've always been,
that turning back does not mean losing ground?
I like it here. I'm lost but, hell, it's green.

Green as a thought, and no-one else around,
which re-minds me. Trivia can mean
common place, something easily found.

II. The Bowl

The pond beside the Bowl we call the 'rusty laptop'
has grown to be less pool than baize pool-tabletop.

A moorhen foots it, Christlike, but for the red dot
that's more a mark of Cain. A football floats to a stop.

It's reached the stage now where to reach the stage is a hop
from the always greener side where grass is smoked and
  cropped

to plant both feet on concrete, almost falling in
love with what was. What is a shelter from the wind,

for watching birds – a hawk, a stonechat, crows, the thin
strut of a heron – watching out for needles and tins,

once hosted Gil Scott-Heron, Stone the Crows, and
  Hawkwind
opening (I swear to God) for Vera Lynn

at a gala fundraiser for – I mean, against – heroin
where the band were reunited with their top

*

-less Irish go-go dancer, Stacia. These days, Stacia
is greatly influenced in her work 'by love of nature,

in all its aspects.' Art-schooled at the Frei Kunstschule,
she grinds up 'landscapes, peoples, animals,' etc.,

into the mix (my laptop's on her Wikipedia).
Like bowerbirds, we gather things that mean together.

Some things go on. The moorhen is a thing that goes
on, not in. Some things just pose and juxtapose

and never break the surface. Some things seem to choose
inertia, having flown, not fallen, out of use.

The Bowl is empty and the Bowl is full. Suppose
I put you in this scene? Suppose that you refuse?

I'd like to think there's time for unbilled cameos,
late entrances, green shoots against rust-red, a future

*

arrives – as parakeets – to say the stage is yours,
Lucia. Green feathers burst into applause.

The Rake Takes His Time

(from you, reader   you'll hardly feel it, but
you'll feel it   a page
is not   a one-way mirror

that papercut
      was not a papercut)

The Rake Regrets To Inform You

and you will be informed by my regret,
rewarded by it. Might we say enriched?

Not like a shrewd investor, more like water
is, to pearl our sharkies fluoride bright.

To form you, I regret. My sacrifice
is like that tooth-white bird who bibs his breast

in red to deem the young – that's you, my dear –
redeemed, reformed. Fed up with re- and in-

formation, I'll regret. Was it the egret,
or the tundra swan? So, set upon

this open bar, my barrel-chest, sate what
we might for want of better words misname

your thirst for *knowledge*, innocency's best
coroner. The cormorant? Oh pet.

'*A sadder and a wiser*' everyone
remembers that bit '*water water*' every

-one recalls '*all creatures great*' etc,
all the creatures, all except the '*Spirit*'

underneath nine fathoms' ice, unholy.
Wholly undescribed except he '*bideth*

by himself' and that until she died
he '*loved*' – another cheap, ill-fitting, flitting

word – that lonely bird, my Laura, Laura
knew her name. I think it rhymed with loss.

The Rake's Looking Glass

Looking very glass indeed.
Wanting nothing, wanting need
and abstinence for once, a seed
of something weak among the weed,
he lets his thoughts lead where thoughts lead:
to Laura, and his one good deed.
Rake turns the other cheek to read
a spiderwebbed yet jangling screed
in lines that crawl his face and breed:
a bleeding heart is prone to bleed
and what's been flayed cannot be fleed
you're in her debt until she's freed
Reflecting on this backwards creed,
he turns to leave. He pays no heed.

His mirrored self kneels down to plead.

The Rake Makes Amends

| a skipping song

one

the rake makes amends
from skin and loose ends
saves them for laura
the lover who lends
a silver dollar
to dance and pretend
he's not not alive

what she would call a
gentleman caller
mr rake is not
hope small   risk smaller
he's all that she's got
what could befall her
there's no second scythe

the dollar she sends
it flickers and bends
in natural light
like all the rake's friends
it doesn't look right
not something to spend
it looks like a knife

rake slips the dollar
under his collar
nicks open a vein

a thin waterfall
to fall for   he drains
his blood   rake falters
falls   opens his eyes

his attic squalor
gone   scratched fats waller
lps and chaise longue
dust and magrittes   all
the here of it gone
the landscape altered
a river of sighs

a land without land
clutched tight in his hand
the bag of amends
exactly as planned
a riverboat wends
its way up the strand
thumb out   hitch a ride

two

boatman smells trouble
rake can befuddle
prestidigitate
meddle and muddle
he tests the coin's weight
scratches his stubble
beckons rake aboard

like milk into ink
a pallid hand slinks
into his pocket
and picks   boatman blinks
an empty socket
the barge almost sinks
try not to rock it
rake's refund secured

watch rake as he goes
with sulfurtipped toes
in high cuban heels
these yellow brick roads
make souls burn   skins peel
but rake's cool as snow
the bricks are confused

whoever paved them
gouged and engraved them
with warped inventions
snares to enslave men
called   *good intentions*
rake never gave them
much notice   his shoes

skip through this unland
exactly as planned
fool bricks underfoot
with tricks underhand
the sky turns to soot

as stone turns to sand
the air is a bruise

rake's getting so close
he hears laura's ghost
not softly sleeping
coyly comatose
but cursing weeping
all mournful-morose
she's howling the blues

three

and here's how it ends
rake lifts the amends
and tendrils of air
fill them end to end
from toenails to hair
merci my old friend
for my birthday suit

her voice clean as stone
like iced honeycomb
Rake's tame as a tomb
and crumbles like loam
remembers the room
where he wanes alone
and looks resolute

a life for a life
that coin like a knife
slits him to pour a
small toast to his wife
laura'd adore a
drop   one would suffice
licks him like a fruit

pomegranate red
her lips where he bled
grow full as rake fades
a flick of her head
shakes warm living shades
of electric thread
stitched from tips to roots

rake wrinkles   dry   wrung
he doesn't have long
as laura escapes
the airless air throngs
with nothings all shaped
like faces rake wronged
betrayed cheated used

a pencilthin line
rake's lips misalign
round one last resort
the ghost of a rhyme
in a book you just bought
the rake takes his time
reader   from   you

Three Poems

NELL PRINCE

The Choice

Which way? Which turn?
I wander through the wood.
I stumble and I learn
paths evil and paths good.
A flutter and a murmur,
a moment that might matter,
I'm lost in whisper, rumour,
I'm last to find my feet.

The Island of San Michele

A graveyard should be ripe –
a breathing, winding plot,
with buzzing, foxglove hype,
all gloom of greenest knot.

Not chapel hollow sleep,
or stony sculptured bed,
or sepulchre too deep
to hide the wormy dead,

but salty winds that shake
the nettles freshly tipped
to sting all ghosts awake
and make a buzzing crypt.

Who wouldn't lie beneath
a plot so humming, housed
by roots that damply sheath
the brain that's wormy-browsed?

Who wouldn't choose this isle
for lying down to rest,
and let the mind awhile
be light and leafy-pressed?

I might have known before
its hidden island's gate,
and shaded, guarded door,
with hopes that come too late,

and smelt the twisted rose
which tangles with the vine,
and heard how silence grows
in flowers full and fine.

East Sands: Different Perspectives

The ocean and the sun are lovers too,
I thought, wondering at the golden blue.
They marry on the edge of morning,
as the first fisherman begins to move
his boat beyond the sunlit cove,
threading the tide along the pier,
from where I watch its ripples smear
the image of the clear light dawning.

The ocean and the sun are strangers too,
I thought, wondering at the misting view,
as certain definitions seemed to vanish,
cathedral spires unraveled and diminished,
silent roads and lanes faded and finished,
drawn inside the haar descending,
around the quay, the town, the sea unending,
until the last of sunlight was extinguished.

Aliens and Ancestors

in conversation with Joyelle McSweeney

OLIVIA MCCANNON

In 'The 'Future' of 'Poetry'', an essay published after the birth of her first daughter, Joyelle McSweeney writes that becoming a mother gave her 'a vision of the present tense in which every moment has its opening on Death'. Far from doomy, this realization led to a sped-up, anachronistic, expanded model of both time and literature where every vista has a sightline on everything else, lit up with both exuberance and dismay.

McSweeney's paradoxical vision of literature lit her way through several books in various genres, including a book of ecopoetics, *The Necropastoral*, which expands on this idea through discussion of poets from Wilfred Owen to Aimé Césaire. But this vision of a link between birth, death, and poetry, was also abruptly and shockingly fulfilled in 2017 with the birth and sudden death of McSweeney's third daughter, Arachne.

Toxicon & Arachne (Corsair, 2021), published in the aftermath of this catastrophe, is McSweeney's fourth book of poems and is her first to appear in the UK. She has called it 'two books that answer each other': the first, obsessed with mutation, contamination, and permutation, was written in the years and months leading up to Arachne's birth; the second, written after her brief life and death, rewrites the first as prophecy. In *Toxicon & Arachne*, grief and damage are simultaneously present in the cellular, collective, and cosmic, in the personal, political, and planetary.

Toxicon sees poetry breaking out of Plato's *Pharmakon*, more poison than cure, verse as virus, Apollo as god of both poetry and plague. At its heart is the virtuosic 'Crown of Toxic Sonnets for John Keats', a sequence whose form feels and makes felt the 'brevity and intensity' of life, with the last line of each sonnet sinking, then resurfacing as the first line of the next; a breath, seeking to catch another breath.

Arachne, named for McSweeney's daughter who died at 13 days old, was written the following spring, from the pain of 'indescribable grief', and out of anger at that season's 'chilly green', that life should return without Arachne.

McSweeney has an interest in the way society punishes those who bring its vulnerabilities into view: 'The obscene is that which should not come to light, but does'. The fearless redress of these poems, is that they move what should not be in the dark, into the sun.

Olivia McCannon: Joyelle, I'm honoured to have this opportunity to welcome Toxicon & Arachne *to these shores, and to have this exchange with you about your work.* Toxicon *is such a dark feast of forms, materials and substances – can I start by asking you about some of the ways in which individual poems took shape in this latest collection? Where did they begin, and how did they go on?*

Joyelle McSweeney: Often, poems I've been really happy with have come in response to unlikely prompts – a request by a friend to remix a poem, or to write a poem on my lunch hour. Those prompts seem to open up a tear in the present tense to make the present-tense even more present, as a more-ness, a spongy, elastic, ungovernable, bouncy material – that is, as sound. Sound pours in through the tear and takes on unanticipatable, ludicrous, arresting shapes. When I perform my poems, I try to reanimate all that sound, send it bouncing through the audience like a thousand hyper little balls.

But even more often, the work that most surprises me, aesthetically and politically, has come about from writing in forms that feel anachronistic – verse plays, sonnet crowns, villanelles, sestinas, or, as in 'Sheep at Derrigimlah', in the Decadent genre of the 'ruined garden' poem. I wrote 'Sheep at Derrigimlah' after visiting the Marconi bog in Connemara. That's where Marconi set up his tower to signal to America, a tower burnt to the ground during the Irish Civil War. Walking along that bog, I felt that burned-down tower bleating to me via the very salty and talkative sheep, and I also felt thronged by restless, livid ancestresses.

OM: There's a line from that poem, 'I am native to this damage', which haunts the book. You've written elsewhere that 'every instant, every cell, is the site of the Anthropocene crisis'. The stratifications of *Toxicon* seem to speak to this acute sense of damage everywhere in space, and matter, but also everywhere in time.

JM: I think the phrase you quote from 'Sheep' really isolates the paradoxical quality of my thinking about time. I'm proposing a denatured version of time in which unpredictable spurts and garrots of anachronistic energy can be released – ravening, mournful, ecstatic, full of voice and information.

Thinking this way brings to mind all kinds of futurisms: the future forced to arrive ahead of time through a summoning of the dead via an intensive, counterintuitive repurposing of what's to hand in the present.

OM: The opening lines of *Toxicon* set its own unique time signature. 'Ah Duralex ah Sominex ah me: | what dream drifts down in time-release?' ('Detonator'). I'm wondering if anachronism has a kind of detonating effect in your poetry, exploding categories of time and scale?

JM: Variations in time and scale go together. The Big Bang triggers change, but the grave can do it, too, and so can the nitrogen vent and the garbage heap. Anachronism can be big, cosmic and showy but it can also be adamantly minute and inward, like the impossible durations, tones and manners of attack proposed in Erik Satie's scores, *like a nightingale with a toothache* – the tiniest trace of a gesture that intervenes in conventional time. The Chilean poet Cecilia Vicuña refers to works of tiny intervention in military, corporate and national time as *precarios.* It is not only humans who can perform such interventions.

I think anachronism, the breaking apart of History, doubling it, caving it in, running it backwards, pressing it flat, stitching it back together in monstrous assemblages, letting other times through, can be and is liberatory, and can be utilized in response to oppressive political structures. I don't think damage is reversible. I don't think we can undo what's been done. But we can jam causality with a preponderance of effects. Like the glittering dresses held up one after the other at the beginning of Kenneth Anger's 'Puce Moment', we can signal towards the dead and the future, the ancestors and the aliens, with whatever material is to hand.

OM: I'm intrigued by these signals, the spirits and energies your poetry seeks to contact. Who or what are the aliens and ancestors that made themselves present to you as you wrote this book?

JM: Well let's begin with Arachne – she was all ways there, ahead of me, behind me, above me, below me, running away with the river and circling back in the rain, falling to earth with the toxic materials. Dead movie stars and pop stars, Leslie Cheung and Kurt Cobain, my secret boyfriend John Keats, Virgil, who taught me how to reach, Cendrars and Breton, all the Surrealists with their slapstick hermeneutics, who taught me how to take down and fold up the rubber horizon and shut it up in a little case that, when you press a little button, goes unfolding and caroming again, spastically and cosmically. Aimé Césaire for the svelteness and fecundity of rage. Hannah Weiner and Alice Notley for their model of poetry as colloquy with other voices, their cosmic (and often comic) inversion of interior and exterior, intimate and profound.

OM: It feels as if your poetry is always mutating and meshing, full of scalar shifts, synaptic leaps and gaps, slippage and streaming, and simultaneity — and always with sound as the energy that breaks and opens what was closed, the transgressive agent that re-fuses the potential radiance of boxed-in words. The structures you make in this way, working the 'toxic and lyric' together, have such integrity, and materiality. Especially as these are the structures of unmaking:

Hunter gatherers: it's come to my attention
a lethality is folded into this scene
as all scenes— it's folded into the eyespots and the
    oxygen rafts
it's folded into the plasmas and the polymers
by which we see, it's folded into the way the universe
blew apart to make a way for us [...]

(From 'Crypt School')

Has your exposure to translated work, or your relationship to hearing, informed the rhythms and tensions of your poetry, in any way?

JM: For ten years now I've been losing my hearing. I have what they call a 'cookie bite' audiogram, because my hearing loss is inconsistent: at certain pitches and volumes, sound suddenly drops away. This has given me a devotion to sound divorced from biological hearing – sound as something mysterious and erratic, suddenly appearing or dropping away.

I've begun to feel like Art is like that too. For years I've been posing myself this question: Where is Art going and Where has it been? How does Art arrive, how can we trace its illimitable Arrivals? This, too, is a question of politics, the spasming of the horizon-line, the caroming departures and returns of the various futurisms – and we (as a planet) need all of them!

But to return to sound: sound drives me, drives the poem, and the words are kind of a collaged attempt to fix the sound in a bouncy structure. I call this kind of writing 'hyperdiction', to draw from what I think Heaney called a 'word hoard' – a souped-up, deluxe, multivalent, hi-lo kind of sound, Virgilian gestures and Looney Tunes acoustics.

OM: Reading *Toxicon and Arachne*, I feel the need to evolve something like 'hyperaudition' to keep up. The space and time of this conversation is running out, and there is so much more I'd love to ask you about, not least the decadent Parisian hauntings of *Toxicon*... Baudelaire, Beckett, Benjamin...? And did I also meet some ghosts from the opening of Cocteau's *Orphée*: 'Behind café glass, | poets clinch and grapple to catch | Death's eye'.

JM: Olivia you are a true dream reader – un vrai Cocteauvian personnage! Eyelids painted on closed eyes surely see further. I think of that brawl at the poets' cafe all the time. Poets want the gods to notice us, it was ever thus, and we'll signal with whatever comes to hand – our poems, our bodies, our lives. Of course, myth instructs that when you actually catch a god's eye, you're in deep trouble. You'll be destroyed. I don't fear that kind of destruction. I'm aiming for it. I'm old-fashioned. An orthodox Decadent. Extremely devout. To quote my own devoutly toxic prayer:

[...] Write me
down, chum me, make me into chyme,
spit me out to lay in sawdust like a germ
then burn me. I release a noxious smell.
Dose me with aminoglycocides
till I give in, then lay me in your litter.
I'm a threat to life.

You know it's funny – I think of myself as a hypercontemporary poet, with holes drilled into me through which all the toxins and intoxicants can run and drain from past to future, from future to past. I've always been drawn to the second part of the Futurist Manifesto, which nobody talks much about, where Marinetti imagines he and his chums sheltering in the wreckage of a crashed airplane and waiting to be torn apart by the Bacchic teens. At the end of *Arachne*, I enact this scene by summoning all my 'vanity virility and fertility/ and crash my plane into the abandoned nursery'. But the nursery is abandoned and it's just me and the plastic Fisher-Price record player playing the novelty hit into eternity. None of us can completely decompose. And so novelty, ephemerality and hyperfatality becomes its own downbeat posthumicity, going on forever, going its inscrutable way.

'Love letters of the Hampstead Modernists' and other poems

FRANCESCA BROOKS

Love letters of the Hampstead Modernists[1]

Love,
    you are pebble-headed
    and starfish-mouthed,
    dark as a lick of brine
    and pocket-smoothed.

That summer
I carried you
       all up the beach,
beloved as an Octopus Rock –
    as if I might taste you
with these fine nerves   *tentacular*
    or come to know you
    as I warmed you in my palm.

Later I prepared a box:
    sea urchin spines, crab
       backs and limp claws,
porcelain-white barnacles
precious as first teeth,
    and most surreal of all –
    the fine armour of
the giant gumboot chiton,
    wingbeats in paralysis.

When I offered it
    you said, Love,
      this is assemblage,
        sculpture,
        collage,
and you gasped.

Hertfordshire Puddingstone

I rise from the fields with the
scorched blue of flint arrowheads,
Thor's unexploded ordnance, the
squid bullets caked with deep clay;
devour all unexplained detritus
from the lost seabed of Hun's Hill
to the backward slopes of Cold
    Christmas.
They call me the breeding stone,
mother of lapidary silica, growing
with the rot of the land, until the plough
cracks at my skull, this rough brain,
crepuscular as fruit pudding baked
under superstition of Ice Age mother-
lodes, sown long before they built
idols into the walls of the parish
church, ashen as unutterable scrolls.

Once I rose up at Chrisall beneath
the Eaves-drip burials, consumed
the chert bones of children, purgatorial
as nested sparrows, dreamt that these
guttered tears would bless me as I
gutted corpses. And I grew bigger
before the rain could baptise them,
lithic as a headstone, voluptuous
as Willendorf – although my flesh
was a conglomerate, a matrix of glass-
eyed flints, they venerated me like
any village pump or war memorial,
the Morris dancers casting May Day
shadows at my hips. What they couldn't
know was this ache: a phantom limb
pulled up from under the dead roots
of the Spinney, a foetal lump, a bear's
lick from the shape it would take above
ground and the hunger that woke it.

1 This poem was inspired by two sets of love letters quoted in Caroline Maclean's *Circles and Squares: The Lives & Art of the Hampstead Modernists*, between Ben Nicholson and Barbara Hepworth, and Paul Nash and Eileen Agar.

The Oak is Down

After Charlotte Mew

In the morning the sky at the window is
a grey-plated etching, spit-bitten but blank,
yearning for line: a texture, a tangle. The
unfretted arc is a flat expanse that cuts
to the heart in grief. All perspective is lost,
all depth.

      The oak is down,
and with it half the spring: this little
ecosystem, days of thought and feeling
projected in its whispering loveliness.
I compose a eulogy of pure sensation
as I make the coffee: that summer haze
of sparkling insects and sun-shocked bugs,
dissolution in bud and greenery, the
lime-green flash of the parakeets, or the
red-crested twist of the woodpecker, the
black, corvid gloss of a pair of ravens, and
the hoot of an owl in the dark, a canopy
above sun-bathing foxes, a yawning bough
for heat-wave weary squirrels. Such an
idyll would have been unimaginable
from a city window. Branches of extended
solace, and the shock of autumn's vibrancy
after weekends away. These images are
cool shivers in a morning turned to mourning.

In the garden all that's left is a fingerprint
of unvarnished oak, a tall wound of mud
and moss where its shadow once stretched,
raw as the leavings of a corpse pulled
through the dirt. After the rain I will count
the tally of its life and think, with regret,
of its executioners, wondering where
they carried the relics, from the roots
to the stem, of that great oak.

A Legend for Hazel

On the day that you are born I am on the dunes at Rosslare
looking out across the grey of the Irish Sea, expecting you.
The messages stop, but I speak of you to the sands and find
two black rocks pressed with the crystal forms of marine fossils.
One speckled as if with iced rain, the other spiral-ribbed
like that rare delicacy, the fiddlehead fern, sought out in the
temperate rainforests of Canada. All things are strange to you,
so I imagine the kind of aunt I might be: remember how this
Christmas, for the first time, Brian's nephew repeated back
to me my own wisdom. *How dead things become rock, once
living things now written in stone.* But it will be several months
before your eyes settle on a colour, and every time we look
at you we will be searching for signs of ourselves, and of
each other, as you dream in blue-green, in deep grey, in hazel
as soft as the silk inside a chestnut shell. Time transforms
in your presence. This is your power already. You are a warm
weight in our arms and the centre of every room. A form
for the future: legs frog-like still, tucked up into you like an
amphibian sprung through algaed water, anxious to find
your shape in the world. When I meet you I think of my
brother as a child. The thought is a photograph: John turning
handstands on the beaches of California, his ribs a pattern
reflected in the ripple of tyre tracks on sand. I wonder if
you will be bowl-cut blonde when that dark, birth hair
grows out, and I remember a thing about my brother that
I had forgotten until now –

Poems from the Pandemic

JUDITH WOOLF

On Reading Li Bai's

Drinking Alone by Moonlight

for Jonathan Sage

Living alone
in the year of the plague,
I no longer drink tea
with my friend and teacher.

Like Li Bai with his winecup,
my companions now
are the moon
and my shadow.

14 April 2020

Advice for Lovers

in the year of the virus
abstinence is safest
if you must embrace

utter no *cries de joie*
share no secretions
and no moist breath

wear a mask and a condom
do not kiss each other
do not lie face to face

after your lover has gone
wipe every surface
rewash the sheets

then cover your face
with your sanitized hands
and weep

21 August 2020

Flattening the Curve

Lockdown,
    shielding,
        easing,
           venturing out.

After months of solitude
           a human touch:

A nurse with a needle kindly taking blood.

6 August 2020

Variations on a Theme

Light through gold leaf
shines green.
The hammer of separation
has beaten it thin.

A hare sits up.
The morning air is chill.
The dancers are sleeping now
under the hill.

24 August 2020

Once more with feeling

Last time the clapping, the rainbows,
The smug community spirit,

Sending each other poems:
'This Lime-Tree Bower My Prison'.

This time we wait for the wave
And hunker down in silence.

'What will be left of the world?'
Sighs a woman walking her dog.

27 September 2020

The Lion of Venice

From the top of his pillar,
The repurposed griffin with the borrowed wings
Views the piazzetta with an agate eye.
Venetian superstition
Says walk between the pillars and you'll die.
Normally, this deters no one,
Since who does not know already they will die?
This year, when masks are not for carnival,
San Marco's crowds are gone.
The lion's eyes, white as a cataract,
Survey blue water edged by empty stone.

1 October 2020

'Hope is the thing with feathers...'

as the days drag by
and the darkness deepens
hope is the feathered thing
that lies plucked and half eaten
once it sang by our window
now maimed and scattered
while we walk on
past its bright wing feathers

in the ear of the mind
 as the darkness deepens
in Messiaen's prison camp
and by Suzee's window
the birds have not ceased to sing
pick up your clarinet
fit a reed on the mouthpiece
hope is a feathered thing

16 October 2020

Retablos

MICHELLE PENN

retablo for the men

they watch from the sidelines, shadow-men, bearded camp
counsellors, jokey dentists she was told she liked, Angel walking the angled
halls of her life, one eye turned to a silhouette, it

jumps at her, the other angel, leaps onto her back, leather wings
thick, inflated muscles fierce, it sinks teeth into her neck, rakes nails across
her face, she heaves it away, stomps its angel foot, plants
a fist into blood-laced lips but it

recovers, it always does, swoops back, wings slapping air, grabs her
shoulders, hisses *I bless you,* yet she's fast as a dancer
sliding down one wing in a tease

while they watch from the sidelines, gentle men, soft men
who meant no harm, *I bless you* the angel hisses, Angel shouts, *No I bless
you*, drowns out the choir of its voice, wipes blood from her neck, straightens
her dress, shadows calling

Angel as she limps down the hallway, keeping one eye
turned to that silhouette, the day begins

retablo for glass

I am a clay pot, raw
  kept from the kiln

a single word
  is water
     beading on my surface
     penetrating the pores

day arrives
  I brace myself, feel it pass
    through skin
and into cells, its sounds bucking, expanding
  every jolt rippling, no gravity to slow it
    I am malleable
  within its boil, the strident greens and bitter purples
     of its spectrum
entire galaxies filter in
  like ghosts as I collect urgencies, count deaths
  my hands shiny
    with the particles of every crisis –

     I am wood
     I am granite
    every surface that seems solid
     I am a faulty membrane
     garden of wreckage
    the mine and the not-mine muddled
       into a single chaotic spur

until the absorption point
until the fullness
until the overspill
  when I become glass

  nothing passes through

    I am not fragile
at least not in any way
    that matters

retablo for the birth of the universe

I don't know who to thank really
  surrounded as I am by atheists
with biblical values so how do I
      track gratitude
especially tiny instants that form monuments
    foxes in doorways
first kisses & the like, normally filed
under *nice*
  but today your mouth & while I
    am too jaded to say it & remain
beneath the book, I simply have to thank
     something

Poems

DAMIAN GRANT

On His Deafness

'No-one has ever written a poem "On His Deafness"' – David Lodge, *Deaf Sentence*

I try to get you side of my good ear;
our conversation gains in clarity,
one might say comprehension. But meanwhile,
what is the bad ear doing? Could it be
that ears are angels, and the evil one
is there to sow dissension, to set down
the stops that make our music? Satan squats
(wrote Milton) at the ear of Eve to spoil
our parents' paradise, and all that is
perverse in us could well find lodging in
the labyrinth of cunning passages
bored in our temples with a stump of wing
to flag the faultline. Or is it the place
set there for love to listen to the things
that Eve and Adam always meant to say?

Storm Light

Today we woke to storm light on the trees
in front of us: birch lit like skeletons,
a haze of early green made luminous,
clouds backing off in panic; and as if
to claim this artwork with its signature
a rainbow bloomed an instant and was gone,
taking the spectacle under its arm.

Manchukuo Journey

SAM ADAMS

i.m. Gareth Jones (1905–35)

5.30 -- morning sun burnishes the palace, swallows taking
breakfast on the wing, slice the haze spread over
Outer Mongolia. At Beidzemiao a living Buddha waits.

Two sentries lean at the gate, one sleeping on his feet,
the other singing to himself, and a woman crouches
over a gaudy headdress strand by strand untangling tassels,
silver discs and trailing coral beads. A small boy limps by.

No map knows the trail we travel, edging the Gobi,
the long way round the sacred mountain. The terrain,
hurls us from side to side, bounces us towards
the creaking car-truck's roof. The desert shudders,
and over all looms Wutaishan, its hundred Buddhist temples.

Will the groaning engine never stop? Have we lost the way?
Then wild thyme strong through open windows, eagles
circle, antelopes cross without a glance, and at the end
of a long ascent plains and ridges stretch ahead for ever.

Midnight, a full moon you might read by and a camel's
skeleton stark in its light, a slink of desert wolves.
Another hour, more, and a town of mud walls and temples,
promises rest. A river bars the way: it takes a bullock team
to drag us up the further bank.

Full morning and a hundred larks give voice, butterflies
and floral meadows, a hillside brown with antelopes, and
soldiers with fixed bayonets guard the streets. Just beyond
the Western gate a poppy field. At the inn a hairless man
boils opium in a frying pan, blows the wood stove
with a Chinese fan, drains slow brown liquid through leaves,
the air a putrid sweetness. Through a curtained doorway,
a rumpled bed, a pipe, a nightmare wait.

Four Sonnets

RACHEL SPENCE

Sonnet for My Mother

Late May 2020, you and your garden
resisting lockdown beneath a thatch of birdsong
bristling with escapee coos, fugitive whistles,
your feral spirit bursting through *coups d'état*
of foxgloves, monkshood, salvia the colour
of pomegranates held by Christ Children,
their mothers gazing forwards to the Passion.
So once you gazed at me, so now I...
No, let's retell. My Madonna is a fighter,
rejecting dead men's histories, watching
lemon light on sapling birches, the golden moss
of bumble bees, their delicate, obsessive turning,
learning to count time as grains that whirl
not flow, spinning us back to love's defiant zero.

8.13am, 18 March 2021, Ludlow.

Ledge days. Leek-white. Unreckoned.
Love thickening like flour and milk
over our low blue heat. *If I hadn't
been an academic, I would have been
a forester.* My father as we walk
the Easy Access Path, my shock salting
the sunlight as it corrugates the pines'
grey verticals. When I tell Mum,
she doesn't blink, her fingers crimping
pastry around the china birds that crown
her favourite pie dish. You dye each other
in a marriage. Take on each other's pigments.
Together you are purple, my king and queen
of pies and dreams. *He's always loved trees.*

Salutation for my Father

7.02am, acne of rain on the window,
rind of cellulite moon. From the kitchen,
Bach's brisk exfoliations whisking me
back to last night as I rose and fell
in candlelit darkness, rootless shadows
begging for a foothold on the flame's
blue yolk. They say you should devote
your practice to someone who needs
your love or energy but in days
with more clamour than stars I pray
for one more morning, one more sonnet,
my father reading Lorca on the sofa,
terrier pooled on his lap like knitting,
his hair so long now, its residue of gold.

Sonnet for Lent (After Beckett)

Hinge week, between equinox
and change of hour. Waking to blue
the colour of stained-glass, tibia of plum,
persimmon. Dawn as free gift. Uncalendared.
By day, I watch you sleep, summoning
your breath like a snake-charmer.
The terrier curled on your chest
like a conch, her tiny body rising
and falling with the ridge and furrow
of your rib-cage. On the edge of a black hole
time stands still. *But the hands of the clock
in the Jewish quarter go to left from right*
And we too choose to live *slowly backwards.*
Not borrowed time but earnt.

Three Poems

CHRISTOPHER RIESCO

Santiago Afternoon

Very sad very sad, the tiles
on the floors are very sad
and the fountains. Fat cabs
with fat drivers leaning out.
Austere official
buildings stand in the sun
that drops at an angle.
The general sweat, Irish,
African, Latin, native,
more in it for the connoisseur
than in any wine cellar,
and all the sun's vineyard anyway.
Facaded townhouses,
hands in their pockets.
Here are some people posed
as if for a photograph, holding up
oranges, bananas, hens,
cigars, bottles of spirit,
sunflowers and lumps of coal,
squinting as if questioning
who you should be,
and why you should want to know.

Real Housework

Real housework is done by
the figure with a palm-frond sweeping
leaves in the Centenario General,
small figure indistinct
in the avenues and avenues.

Real birthday presents are given
by those accustomed
leaving fresh flowers in the basins
and real conversation is held
by old ladies talking into the air.

Out in the backwoods it goes on
a heavy stone is placed on top of the
tomb, to keep down the lid, a kind
shush finger on the lips to calm
those that cry out
for the real sweets of the resurrection.

By contrast the halfway house where
I live is affable and slutty. No real
work is done, only breathing and eating,
and casual rest.

This Old Wick

The evening of the spirit, then
sets on slower and firmer than
the evenings of the sun and world
which flicker in your eyes while
this old wick crumbles in your head
and the yesterday wax sets rigid.

Who's in the bamboo? Poison-
tipped arrows and mud on your face,
naked, with sharpened teeth.
Who dances around a log
carved into a dozen contorted faces
and draws harsh notes from the bamboo.

Curtain opens on a still feast,
silver plate, game with feathers,
grapes, fluted cups, a dulcimer,
all too still, one thing moving
shiny and black, the hiss the only sound,
the candle-light shimmering on the scales.

Reviews

'ogh ogh ogh bum'

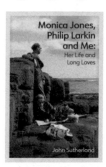

John Sutherland, *Monica Jones, Philip Larkin and Me: Her Life and Long Loves* (Weidenfeld & Niicholson) £20
Reviewed by Ross Cogan

There's something about genius – especially early-flowering genius – that can distort the mind. You often see it in the best chess players, who can become Grandmasters in their early teens. It's as if so much skill, so narrowly focused, can't exist in the brain without stunting its other faculties. At the extreme end you get Bobby Fischer with his infantile tantrums, conspiracy theories and anti-Semitism.

There was something of the Grandmaster in Philip Larkin. His genius only worked in a highly structured, rigorously rule-bound environment. He would work on poems slowly and meticulously, saving up a choice word as you might a new line in the Najdorf, knowing that you could only play it once before the surprise was lost. And his talent started blooming early – the juvenilia he wrote at sixteen is better and more interesting than most poets' mature work.

But as his genius developed the rest of him atrophied. Emotionally he seems to have changed little after 1940, except to get gloomier, and to the end of his life was happiest in a world of Armstrong's Hot Five, Willow Gables, Dexter and Compton, dirty mags, and 'ogh ogh ogh bum' with Kingsley. A lot of people have given a lot of time to trying to understand Larkin's emotional depths, motivations and relationships (and not just with women – Richard Bradford devoted an entire book to his relationship with Amis). Were he and Monica co-dependent? Was he 'coercively controlling'? I would respectfully suggest that this is a pointless exercise. In my opinion the shallows just hide more shallows; ultimately Larkin was a clever teenager inhabiting the body of a provincial librarian.

Men like this struggle with complex, demanding women. And for men of his type and generation there was only one solution – run away and hope they get the message. Usually they did. Ruth Bowman got the message, despite having been engaged to him, and so did Patsy Strang. But then naïve Ruth and alcoholic Patsy both had more emotional intelligence than Monica Jones. When Kingsley Amis famously lampooned her as Margaret Peel in *Lucky Jim* he described her as 'adhesive' and whatever you feel about the rest of the portrait, with that adjective the Old Devil hit the nail on the head. When Larkin fell out of love with her – I guess in the late 50s – and ran away, Monica followed. And so the pattern was established for the rest of their lives – Philip putting (physical and emotional) space between them, being unkinder, ruder and surlier; Monica becoming more and more abject and querulous, and living for the trip to the test match, the annual holiday on Sark and one weekend in four.

And, of course, the letters. Philip and Monica wrote regularly to each other from 1946 until 1973 when the telephone took over. Larkin wrote regularly to almost everyone he knew – at least that's how it sometimes seems. His *Letters to Monica* were edited by Anthony Thwaite and published in 2010. John Sutherland is the first scholar to have carefully and comprehensively reviewed Jones's letters (not, as some reviewers have claimed, the first to be given access to them – Thwaite quotes from them too) – housed in 54 boxes in the Bodleian – and they form the bedrock of his biography.

Sutherland approached them with a clear intention – to rescue Monica's reputation for posterity. He was taught by Jones as both an undergraduate and postgraduate at Leicester and became a friend as well as a protégé – one of her 'boys' who she drank with in the pub. Stung by the chorus of taunts she has received – 'a grim old bag' (Amis, K), 'real butch… a *beast*' (Amis, M), 'frigid, drab and hysterical' (Christopher Hitchens), 'possibly even a man in drag' (AN Wilson) 'built like a scary Brünnhilde' (Maureen Paton) – as well as the unflattering literary portrayals (not just as Margaret Peel, but also Viola Masefield in Malcolm Bradbury's *Eating People is*

Wrong) he sets out to rehabilitate the brilliant, warm, flamboyant teacher that he knew. Sadly, he fails.

It should be noted that he was on a losing wicket. Indeed, the very attempt is brave to a degree that says much for Sutherland's sense of loyalty. Monica is not an easy person to defend, particularly at the moment, and almost the first point that every reviewer has raised is her racism, homophobia and anti-Semitism. Sutherland admits that he knew something of this while he was studying with her, but didn't appreciate the scale. The 'casually venomous' anti-Semitism, in particular, he found went beyond anything in Larkin's writing, while there is enough racism – something Sutherland calls the 'N-word song' stands out – to get you cancelled before you could say 'At Grass'.

If anything, the situation is worse than Sutherland suggests. In an early letter (5 August 1953), Larkin explains away a quarrel by saying that, though not very political, he naturally sides with the left ('I certainly *never* knew you fancied yrself a Socialist' said Jones on 30 July, in a letter Sutherland doesn't quote but Anthony Thwaite does). The young Larkin, like the young Amis, was left wing, perhaps in reaction to his (literally) fascist father. Of course, Larkin knew little about politics and cared less. He would inevitably have drifted rightwards over time under the influence of Amis and Bob Conquest. But Amis was never racist – quite the reverse: while teaching at Vanderbilt University, Nashville in 1967 he was so shocked by the treatment of black people that he viciously satirised his hosts in *I want it Now*. So we have to consider the possibility that Monica's influence was responsible for the ugly character of Larkin's later views.

As if this weren't bad enough, it's hard to sympathise much with a woman confronting misogyny when, as Blake Morrison rightly notes in the *Guardian* 'she was a bit of a misogynist herself'. Appointed in 1946 as only the second member of the Leicester English department, she was still the only woman when Sutherland arrived in 1960 – never a feminist, she had done nothing to secure the appointment of other women, delighting in her unique status. Never promoted above the rank of lecturer, she saw colleagues repeatedly appointed over her head. However Sutherland tacitly admits this was largely her own fault, as she refused to publish, claiming to find it 'showy', and preferring to spend her long vacations holidaying, gardening and – later – drinking.

Sutherland makes some half-hearted attempts to defend her from the implication that she was bone idle. She did publish, he claims, 'she merely did it her way', by which he means that she was responsible as co-author for Larkin's *Oxford Book of Twentieth-Century English Verse*. This was a 'Larkin-Jones map of twentieth century poetry' and by placing her first in the acknowledgements Larkin accepted that 'she could have been on the title page'. This rather ignores the fact that it was Larkin who spent long hours in the Bodleian researching it. No doubt Monica did much to shape his taste, and perhaps also made material contributions, but by that account Larkin's name could have been on the title page of *Lucky Jim*. Moreover, if we accept Sutherland's claim then it does Monica no good, since what he doesn't mention is

that the 'Bloody OxBo' was full of mistakes, including the omission of half of Empson's 'Aubade' and the last two verses of Thom Gunn's 'The Byrnies'. 'I can see myself joining Bowdler and Grainger' Larkin wrote to Thwaite, 'to *Larkinize*, v.t., to omit that part of a poem printed on verso and subsequent pages'. These, of course, are exactly the sort of mistakes that a good academic should have spotted.

It gets odder. Sutherland complains that, while her failure to gain promotion was probably fair – 'Miss Jones did not do what she was paid to do and took half the year off not to do it' – nonetheless an exception 'should have been made, because Monica Jones was exceptional. Which of her colleagues is in the *Oxford Dictionary of National Biography* for services to literature?', which looks bizarrely close to suggesting that academic preferment might legitimately depend on who you know.

The worst thing about this book, though, the really unforgiveable thing, is that it is dull. Looking back on her life at the age of 76, Monica told James Booth that 'I found it *terribly boring* actually'. Sutherland should have taken the hint. Instead he makes the classic biographer's mistake – let loose on an unexplored source (those 54 boxes) he was jolly well going to make the most of them, regardless of content. So we learn that at Christmas 1965 she 'had a vast clear up of the kitchen', that she believed she always looked good in trousers, what she was cooking, where she was holidaying and that South Africa played at Lords in 1965 ('England are headed by two of the country's most boring batsmen: Tom Graveney and Ken Barrington'. Actually this is wrong – Graveney wasn't picked for the South Africa series. Perhaps he's confusing him with Geoff Boycott.)

We also learn about her immediate family – devout Methodists on both sides and also dull (Monica complained to Sutherland 'over jars in the Clarendon' that George Eliot was 'a writer who should only be read by Methodists on wet Sunday afternoons' – another hint he should have taken). And all this is accompanied with lashings – literally – of querulous and often self-coruscating complaints ('I dread the whole rest of my life', 'I hated my birthday, walked the streets all the afternoon', 'I'm surprised and disappointed by myself', 'I think I feel as very old people must feel'.)

The really tragic thing is that Monica Jones was clearly an inspiring lecturer and an intelligent, exceptionally well-read woman with forthright views. There was a good book waiting to be written here. But it wasn't a conventional biography – her life just wasn't interesting enough to warrant one. Instead Sutherland should have written a genuine memoir – concentrated on the woman he knew, her personality, her ideas, her wit, her views of literature – particularly her views of literature, since this is what actually made her interesting, and enabled her to play a role in shaping Larkin's verse.

The hints we get of these are tantalising, but hints are all they are. There are some fascinating comments on *Hamlet*, and, of course, Hardy, but I wanted more. Why, for example, are Thackeray, Austen, Scott and Trollope 'gold in your pocket for life'? What is so wonderful about George Crabbe and William Barnes? Why were Yeats and DH Lawrence 'silly' and Ted Hughes 'moving towards silliness'? 'Her *Vanity Fair* lecture made me a Thackerayan for life' he says. 'I hear her in my mind as I write her loud clear voice ... inflecting itself to uncover the sexually hinted innuendos which only an ear attuned to the clubman Thackerayan voice could catch as they wafted, tobacco-laden into print.' That's great, John, but what did she actually *say*?

Sutherland could, in short, have sketched an outline of the book that Jones never wrote. And if his own memory and Monica's letters didn't provide enough evidence, then he could have interviewed former colleagues and students – Monica only retired in 1982, there should be many students alive and some of them may even have their lecture notes.

What will survive of us isn't love, it's – at least in those rare cases where anything survives – words. Sutherland had a chance to save Monica's best words, her views on Thackeray, Shakespeare, Hardy, Scott and Crabbe. Instead he chose 'had a vast clear up of the kitchen', 'I dread the whole rest of my life' and the N-word song. Poor Monica. In the end, her friends served her no better than her enemies.

Questions from the Edge

Kate Kirkpatrick, *Becoming Beauvoir: A Life* (Bloomsbury Academic) £20; Peter Salmon, *An Event, Perhaps: A Biography of Jacques Derrida* (Verso) £16.99
Reviewed by Nicolas Tredell

The subjects of these informed and lucid biographies, Simone de Beauvoir and Jacques Derrida, can serve to represent two key moments in twentieth-century French intellectual life – existentialism and deconstruction – which had an impact far beyond France but which can now seem, to borrow a phrase from Donald Davie's poem 'Remembering the 'Thirties', 'more remote than Ithaca or Rome', belonging to those foreign countries of the relatively recent past that can appear more distant than those farther back in time. It is not that the ideas developed in those moments have wholly disappeared but rather that, like the ideas of psychoanalysis, they have been domesticated, simplified, popularized and assimilated into quite different contexts. In a sense, we are all existentialists and deconstructionists now.

Both biographies aim to stress above all the philosophical concerns of their subjects, even if they have, for differing reasons, been denied philosophical respectability in some quarters. Derrida and Beauvoir were both steeped in previous philosophy and their ideas emerged out of and against this. As Beauvoir declared in a 1947

article, 'it is indispensable to be familiar with the long tradition on which it rests if one wants to grasp both the foundations and the originality of the new [philosophical] doctrine'. While 'foundations' and 'originality' are suspect terms from a deconstructionist perspective, Salmon contends that Derrida's work 'often appears to assume a thorough working knowledge of most of the history of Western philosophy' as well as much else. Both Beauvoir and Derrida were also steeped in literature and their philosophical explorations took literary forms, even if Derrida never ventured into fiction.

One of the most interesting aspects of Kirkpatrick's account of Beauvoir's philosophical development, however, is its attention to lesser-known thinkers whom she encountered in her early studies. There was, for instance, Claude Bernard, whose *Introduction à l'étude de la médecine expérimentale* (1865) she commended, in an essay written when she was sixteen, for its positive valuation of 'fertile doubt', 'that philosophical doubt which leaves to the mind its freedom and initiative'. Then there was Alfred Fouillée, whose *La Liberté et le déterminisme* (1890) contended, contra Rousseau, that 'Man isn't born, but rather becomes free' – an assertion that Beauvoir would echo and adapt in *Le Deuxième Sexe* (1949) in her most famous axiom: 'One is not born, but rather becomes, a woman' (*On ne naît pas femme: on le devient*'). Even in writers and thinkers steeped in canonical works, relatively marginal texts may fruitfully fuel their intellectual development.

A biographical interest in Beauvoir seems to flow naturally from her own copious autobiographical writings. Salmon's biography of Derrida, however, may appear alien to its subject's philosophical approach, creating a coherent linear narrative out of a discontinuous heterogeneity of deconstructible events. In contrast, Beauvoir's life-writings do present a largely coherent narrative and create a potent image of herself and Sartre that has subsequently been challenged, not least by Beauvoir herself in her posthumously published letters and diaries. While she never claimed to tell the whole truth in her autobiographies, practising a reticence partly prompted by the fact that key figures who featured in it were still living and partly by a desire to present an exemplary life lived beyond conventional limits, we now know of striking omissions and discrepancies; in particular, her sexual relationships with younger women, all former students – Olga Kosawiecz, Bianca Bienenfeld and Nathalie Sorokine, whose mother lodged a debauchery charge, never confirmed, against her daughter's teacher.

In terms of Beauvoir's relationships with men, her congress with Sartre, while intellectually and emotionally intimate and enduring, never seems to have reached sustained erotic heights, and physical relations between them petered out after ten years or so. Her fulfilling heterosexual relationships were with Jacques-Laurent Bost, who would later marry Olga; with Nelson Algren, her 'beloved Chicago man', who gave her a cheap Mexican ring that she wore for the rest of her life and that was buried with her; and with Claude Lanzmann, the only man with whom she ever cohabited – for seven years – and the only one she ever addressed with the familiar '*tu*'. As Kirkpatrick observes, 'evaluating Beauvoir's life seems to require the forcible displacement of Sartre from the centre'.

Derrida, by contrast, seems to have led a largely blameless bourgeois life, marrying Marguerite Aucouturier, a translator and later a psychoanalyst and having two sons, Pierre and Jean. There was one consequential deviation, however: an affair, begun in 1972, with Sylviane Agacinski, then twenty-seven, who would go on to produce several books on gender, literature and philosophy and to marry the future French prime minister, Lionel Jospin. In 1978 and 1984, Sylviane became pregnant; the first time this happened, she had an abortion but on the second occasion she gave birth to a boy, Daniel, whom Derrida's wife persuaded him to acknowledge as his own, though he seems to have had little to do with his upbringing. Of course, this chain of events could have been easily accommodated among the *bien pensant* French bourgeoisie of the nineteenth century and was even more acceptable among the progressive French bourgeoisie of the twentieth. In worldly-wise mode, Salmon suggests that '[b]ack in 1980, the relationship [with Agacinski] was in the midst of the frantic stage which characterises any affair' and then falls into vulgar autobiographical speculation by contending that this amorous agitation informs Derrida's *The Post Card: From Socrates to Freud and Beyond*, a work 'written in the form of postcards, or *envois*, sent by a man to his lover' which 'does seem painfully autobiographical'. Sylviane almost becomes Derrida's dark lady.

The most interesting biographical element of Salmon's biography, and the one we can most plausibly relate to Derrida's ideas, is its account of his complex childhood, adolescence and young adulthood. An interesting harbinger of onomastic difference appears on his birth certificate; his given forename was 'Jackie', apparently after Jackie Coogan, the child star of Charlie Chaplin's film *The Kid* (1921), and in this beginning was his end; 'Jackie' is incised on his gravestone. He was born on 15 July 1930 in Algiers, into a Sephardic Jewish family, ten days after the celebration of a century of French colonial rule that was to explode, in the 1950s, into a violent conflict in which Derrida, like Camus, found himself uncomfortably torn between his emancipatory principles and *pied noir* family sympathies. As Derrida himself put it, in a late interview quoted by Salmon, he grew up 'a sort of child in the margins of Europe, a child of the Mediterranean, who was not simply French nor simply African, and who passed his time traveling between one culture and the other feeding questions he asked himself out of that instability'. It does seem reasonable to link this biographical marginality with Derrida's development of a manner of thinking and writing that engaged with European philosophy but also questioned it from the edge – and here also, perhaps, is the link, across many differences, with Beauvoir. Born and brought up in Paris, in the metropolitan centre, she progressed through the élite institutions to which her intelligence and industry gave access; but her status as a woman still marginalized her and made her develop a way of thinking and writing that, from the edge, asked awkward questions.

Then is Now

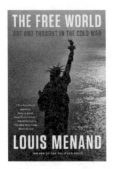

Louis Menand, *The Free World: Art and Thought in the Cold War* (Farrar Straus and Giroux) £23.10
Reviewed by Tony Roberts

James Russell Lowell sounded a note of caution when he wrote in 1867, 'our culture is, as for a long time it must be, European; for we shall be little better than apes and parrots till we are forced to measure our muscle with the trained and practised champions of that elder civilization'. He could hardly have guessed just how much muscle the USA would be able to flex in Europe within a century, militarily, economically and artistically.

World War 11 brought isolationist America back to world affairs for the second time in forty years, ending the Depression. Peace, however, meant only a new front, the Cold War, which was to hamper the nation's psyche. This was the time, as Jill Lepore argued in *These Truths* (2018), 'when the United States built a national security state' because of its fear of Communism, and thus 'a peace dividend expected after the Allied victory in 1945 never came'. What came instead were cagey, proxy confrontations and years of aggressive rhetoric. It was a time of seriousness of purpose, but of devastating ill-judgement abroad (the Cold War, Vietnam) and at home (McCarthyism, institutional sexism, racism and homophobia). Beneath the conservatism of the period, cultural historians like Morris Dickstein (*Leopards in the Temple*, 2002), detected an energy radically at odds with conformism, initially manifest in literature and film, which would be given dramatic expression in the 1960s.

It is this postwar period that Louis Menand has chosen to document in *The Free World: Art and Thought in the Cold War* and he has done it splendidly, in a work epic in both ambition and achievement. Menand is a respected observer of the American historical scene, a Harvard exponent of intellectual history and culture, as compulsively readable as, say, our own Stefan Collini. Known widely for his pieces in *The New Yorker*, *The New Republic* and *The New York Review of Books*, he is also the author of *Discovering Modernism: T. S. Eliot and His Context* (1987), his Pulitzer prizewinning study of pragmatism, *The Metaphysical Club* (2001) and a collection of essays, *American Studies* (2002).

Reading his new book, one is reminded of Benedetto Croce's dictum 'all history is contemporary history'. Under the destructive years of the last presidency, America practised a trumpeting, aggrieved and predatorial isolationism. This is perhaps the spur to *The Free World*. 'This book,' it begins, 'is about a time when the United States was actively engaged with the rest of the world.'

In his preface, Menand sets out his stall. His focus is on the twenty years post-1945 when American dollars, via the Marshall Plan, helped regenerate war-ravaged Europe – at a price: the exportation of liberal democracy, American style. His intention is to explore the underlying social forces and the resultant cultural terrain by taking 'a series of vertical cross-sections', focusing on leading practitioners in their fields (almost exclusively men, given the times). For all its 'free world' emphasis, this is a book chiefly about American experience.

Menand is keen to stress that 'the existence of the Cold War was a constant but only one of many contexts' in his book. These contexts tended to produce cultural goods which, like Abstract Expressionism, could anyway be seen as capitalist propaganda, as instruments of Cold War foreign policy. Writing of the source of Pop Art, he observes that people had been taught 'to think of modern art as a story with a single narrative whose stages developed internally... Painters X did this, which led painters Y to do that'. He avoids the approach, offering various narratives, linking contexts, themes and characters.

Among the most interesting of these are: Kennan and 'containment', the political manoeuvring that became the Cold War; the slow death of institutional anti-Semitism in American academia; scientific racism, civil rights and the fight for a black identity; the emergence of dissonance in dance, art and music; censorship and the paperback revolution; sexism versus second-wave feminism; Hollywood Americana and the influence of *La Nouvelle Vague*; and the Vietnam War's politicizing of students at home.

To take just one thread as an illustration: 'Freedom and Nothingness' (Chapter 3), concerns a Paris well-known to us through the work of writers such as Robert Gildea, Julian Jackson, Tony Judt and Sarah Bakewell, and yet still Menand turns up eye-opening details which may not have lodged earlier, such as the fact that most of the Free French divisions were a majority non-white, hence Leclerc's Second Armoured Division (75% white) was chosen to liberate Paris. Similarly, he gives a context for de Gaulle's fears of the ongoing influence of the French Communist Party (the PCF) – recognized for its wartime resistance – in reminding us that postwar it had twelve daily newspapers and forty-seven weeklies in its control.

He then turns to Paris's intellectual star of the period, Jean Paul Sartre (who could do a great Donald Duck impersonation, as we learn from one of Menand's ironic digressions). Sartre's resistance credentials were underwritten by his belief that almost all French people had been *résistants* in wartime ('a free act made in the name of freedom, whatever the act is and whoever makes it, is by its nature an act of resistance'). Inevitably many celebrated figures have only walk-on parts: Camus and Paulhan in Paris, for instance, Aron in London and Benjamin, dying in Port Bou. He has more to say on Hannah Arendt, who recognized in flight that 'The European tradition had destroyed itself' and who finally escaped to America to find – as Alexander Herzen had found in London in the previous century – that her adopted nation offered the protection of its institutions, but a conformism that stultified.

Most interesting here, perhaps, are Menand's comments concerning the French take on American fiction, an influence on Existentialism. He introduces the reader to Maurice-Edgar Coindreau, whose impact 'was enormous, not only on the Americans he translated, particularly Faulkner, whose French reception was almost certainly crucial to his receiving the Nobel Prize in 1949, but also on French literary culture itself'. As Menand explains, French translation 'largely bleached out markers of race, region, and class' in their novels. 'The effect was to classicize.' Influence came down to a matter of time displacement and characterization. From the movies (and *vice versa*) Americans had learnt to play with narrative (flashback, montage, techniques of ellipsis) and to focus on exteriority, on action rather than on analysis of character motive.

Menand practises a revealing dualism with his vast cast of characters: Orwell and Burnham , Baldwin and Wright, Cage and Cunningham, Friedan and Beauvoir, Rauschenberg and Johns, Trilling and Ginsberg, Langlois and Bazin, Warhol versus the *avant-garde*, and so on.

He has an eye for stripping off the mythical accretions on anecdotes. He does this with Kerouac's *On the Road*. Apparently, Kerouac was not actually making the novel up at the keyboard after being inspired by a letter from Neal Cassady, as is often told, but working from drafts and journals. Nor was he typing – as the image has it – on a continuous roll of teletype paper, but on ten twelve-foot rolls of drawing paper. Also, Cassady's letter itself was inspired by one from John Clellon Holmes.

Elsewhere Menand recounts the formative experience Isaiah Berlin had in visiting the officially disgraced poet Akhmatova in Moscow in 1956 (her 'guest from the future'), revealing the implausibilities in the romanticized version of their meeting. The elisions in Berlin's account(s) were meant to protect this ideological enemy of the state. And yet the line 'She was a seducer, but so, very much, was he', reads a tad steamy for Berlin-watchers.

Similarly, when Menand writes of Orwell: 'He turned his life into an experiment in classlessness', he is telling half a story. He might have added that despite his rough living, the Etonian Orwell had a problem with this. As his niece recalled, 'I think a lot of Eric's [Orwell] hang-ups came from the fact that he thought he ought to love all his fellow-men; and he couldn't even talk to them easily.'

Finally, because Menand *is* so generously inclusive, we begin to miss people: we have Sontag but hardly the similarly abrasive Mary McCarthy; Cleanth Brooks is here but barely Allen Tate, one of the great networkers. Further, certain figures who seem to have had an impact on the culture of the period, at the time, are missing: Charlie Parker, Arthur Miller, Fred Zinnemann, John Wayne, to name a few. But then that is a game the reader can enjoy indulging in.

One salient remark in *The Free World* – a book full of them – comes from Susan Sontag. In an interview for *The Paris Review* (1994) she said, 'I was assuming that a principal task of art was to strengthen the adversarial consciousness.' Menand's book illustrates just how and how many artists in all media felt this to be their mission.

Taxonomy

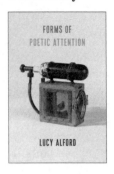

Lucy Alford, *Forms of Poetic Attention*
(Columbia University Press), £54 (hb), £25 pb
Reviewed by Chris Miller

68 Reviews

Forms of Poetic Attention is a very ambitious book. It might best be described as an Aristotelian attempt to tabulate the forms of poetic attention as these are exhibited in the poem. It derives from a study of attention in ethics and the question: where can we practice disinterested intention? Is there a body of literature 'giving voice to attention'? The result is not only a study of attention in poetics but a series of philosophically-informed close readings, structured in illustration of those forms.

To begin with Alford's framework: her study is in two parts, dealing respectively with Transitive and Intransitive Attention. The former is considered under what Alford calls its Dynamic Coordinates: Interest (desire, for example, contrasted with a more disinterested attention), Intentionality (deliberate attending or attention caught), Selectivity, Temporal Remove and Apprehension (or 'capture': does the object come to life?). Within Selectivity, the poem may show greater or lesser degrees of Concentration (Dickinson compared to Charles Wright), Resolution (zooming in or out) and Integrity (the object of attention may be entire or divided). We are then invited into the Modes of Transitive Attention: Contemplation, Desire, Recollection, and Imagination. This is a meal in itself. It will immediately strike the reader that these are large categories; the extent of the book is required for Alford to do justice to the intermingling and *recoupements* of these coordinates and modes; their initial statement inevitably has some of the qualities of certain Aristotelian dicta midway between the self-evident and the revelatory such as 'By 'whole' I mean 'with a beginning, a middle and an end' in the *Poetics*.

In the second half of the book, Intransitive Attention has its own Dynamic Coordinates: Intentionality, Presence of an Indirect Object (the object of an object of meditation is, in meditation, that it should be transcended), Scope (which is like Selectivity), Temporal Inflection, and Subjectivity (in particular the unselving of ecstasy), and is offered the Modes of Vigilance, Resignation, Idleness and Boredom.

This very bald introduction to the book's aims may make it seem at once finical and suspect, which it is not; thus, her four modes of transitive attention, Alford says, 'offer, much like primary colours, a basic, skeletal, and infinitely combinatory model'. Alford is aware that her categories are the barest bones of a complex organism.

One of the first things to say about her book is that almost everything in it is neatly and often memorably articulated ('The problem of form is, at root, the problem of contingency'; 'The poem calls itself out of the blank noise to give itself form'). It is a book written by a poet of athletic intellectual attainment and its sentences are logically and rhythmically coherent to a degree that literary scholarship rarely attains. Nothing could be less dogmatic. Though the book is rich in attention and cognitive studies, its venture is not, as Structuralism was, scientistic. Reading it as yet another technology of interpretation does it an injustice. It is best understood as a particularly subtle account of the modalities of reading, bringing to bear a remarkable range of scientific, philosophical, theoretical and critical reading on a very wide range of poems. (One of the pleasures of Alford's writing is the ease with which she is able to turn aside from her taxonomy and map it onto the history of philosophy.)

Her distinction of transitive and intransitive attention is not in itself revelatory or indeed decisive, nor are the dynamic coordinates that she proposes. But, meshing with her modes and exercised in her range of close readings, they begin to bear fruit. Though her topics may seem philosophically arduous and do indeed call for sustained attention, her tone is never didactic: 'I consider the structures I unfold to be invitations for further investigation and attention'. At every point, she does philosophical justice to the categories she proposes: 'With the poem's composition of a semantic object, the imaginative faculty of mental representation is called upon to build in the mind a simulated experience of perception. Even the most direct observational impulse, the most faithful realism, is composed in and of the imagination'. Her close readings are fully informed by both the literature and, where available, the theorisations of the poet; this is particularly true of her readings of Stevens. Her introduction to Contemplation in Transitive Attention moves easily between Aristotle and Buddhism, passing through Weil, Malebranche and George Herbert before arriving at her illustrative selection: Ponge, Heaney, Stevens and Elizabeth Bishop. And the poetry sampled in the book ranges from the Ancient Egyptian, Sappho and pre-Islamic Arabic to Alford's Anglophone contemporaries; it includes poets like Joan Retallack, described under Idleness, whose 'procedural errancy' is 'causative' and 'interventionist', since generated by numerical constraints of Oulipesque kind. Alford is not deterred, as I am, by the 'near-total lack of semantic figuration in these lines', which 'prohibits meaning-making'. Retallack's work, essentially Conceptual, obviously constitutes a more interesting object of study under the focus of attention studies than to those seeking imaginative identification with poetry.

The poems selected almost invariably justify their place in the structure of her argument and her historical range is also pleasurable; it is a delight to find her, shortly before establishing Heaney as a champion of 'apprehension' in the 'immediacy of [his] imagery', quoting Sidney ('many of such writings as come under the banner of unresistible love, if I were a mistress, would never persuade me they were in love') to show that 'apprehension is not about thick description or analysis'. It might then seem unfair to say that Ponge and Heaney are rather obvious candidates for this category, since that is the function assigned to them. And it is typical that Alford lists a number of other poets whom she might have chosen, as various as Wordsworth, Bonnefoy and Darwish, and emphasises the point that apprehension 'depends on the particularity of the reader and the reading moment'. Each close reading is bound to generate its own response in her reader, a point she would surely relish; my copy is stuffed with print-outs of all the poems not given in extenso. For example, in her brief account of Heaney's 'Oysters', I feel Alford fails to register the import of the poet's mythological references. When the next line is 'Alive and violated', it is important to know that 'As I tasted the salty Pleiades / Orion dipped his foot into the water' is a reference to rape and harassment vested in the very cosmology of the season's constellations.

Her chapter on 'Poetry, Painting and Learning How to See' is a notably rich exemplification of her proceeding. It begins with a Merritt Chase painting 'befriended at the Art Institute of Chicago', quotes Mark Doty on the 'tenderness' of being 'held within an intimacy with the things of the world', contemplates Bishop's 'The Fish', goes back to Doty ('A language of ideas is, in itself, a phantom language'), observes 'Things matter – they are our neighbours, our others...', examines the 'double relationality' of ekphrasis, notes that, in poetic contemplation, 'The poem is not a record of a past event of perception, or a representation of a past object, but an event of perception in itself'; adds that 'total capture of the thing' is unattainable, but that the aim of contemplation is not total capture but 'being with, being alongside, and *staying* with'. The favoured environments for the *via contemplativa* (libraries, galleries) are not always available or even helpful; 'most of us...may not even feel welcome in them' – though this 'us' may lie well outside her readership. She then looks at the work of Harryette Mullen, *Urban Tumbleweed*, as an example of contemplative practice 'in the thick of urban life' (Mullen takes her cue from Bashō in her regular walks); quotes Janet Hirshfield on writing poetry as a 'contemplative practice', cites Kierkegaard on the speech of the poet', so 'solemn' that it is 'almost like silence', and to which silence might be preferable, and concludes by considering the 'active focus and passive reception' required in contemplative poetry. Hard not to learn something here. To begin with, I had never heard of Mullen, whose work I should like to explore.

Alford is particularly good on Intransitive Attention. Her modes are nicely defined: Vigilance is a 'state of attention in which there is no present object of focus, but rather an openness to *potential* objects'. Resignation is 'a release from an interested, transitive attending into a non-attached, disinterested attention...Like vigilance, resignation occupies a particular – necessarily *present* – temporality. But, unlike vigilance...the present of this particular mode of intransitivity is one that is inflected by the shadow of the past, the shadow that remembers what has been let go'. Attention is 'colloquially synonymous with only one of its many aspects, that of focalized attention' and thus 'to think of states like boredom and idleness as modes of attention might seem oxymoronic', but in both 'the attention is passively present without focalized engagement'. In idling, 'there is an acceptance,

even an embrace, of the unstructured attentional state, while in boredom there is an unhappy consciousness of the lack of engagement paired with an inability or unwillingness to engage'. Science, she tells us, now links 'task-negative' modes of attention to the 'default mode network' characteristic of a mind not engaged in 'intentional executive tasks'. The poems of idleness analysed are by Retallack, O'Hara and Ammons; those of boredom Bukowski, Gunn and Eliot. There is no great paradox here; we are familiar with the poetry, indeed the literature, of ennui, from Baudelaire to Laforgue and from *A Hero of our Time* to Maria Edgeworth's recipe for escape-from-unfeeling-tedium to bourgeois-careerism-with-the-right-woman-at-the-end-of it in, yes, *Ennui*. Alford's account of Rimbaud under Resignation may seem paradoxical, such is the energy of his words, but it is very convincing and summarised in her section title, 'From the poetry of resignation to the resignation of poetry'. Charles Wright is her poet of 'resignation as meditation'; this is a poetics with which she is clearly in deep sympathy and one of his poems is the starting point for her introduction.

Reviewing the book in the *Wallace Stevens Journal* (45.1), Zachary Finch describes Alford's framework as not just that of a 'taxonomist, with pretensions to totality, but of a curator, whose speculative groupings and classifications are themselves a kind of art': 'it feels as if Alford is a knowledgeable docent walking us from room to room in some immense Met or Louvre'. The analogy is apposite in terms of the historical sweep of the book and this, in turn is possible because the focus is on attention, which is so fundamental not only to reading but to intellection of any kind, however passive. A poem is best understood as 'an instrument for tuning and composing the attention'. And 'poetic attention' is not just attention to poetry but 'modes of attention that function poetically', that is, in a non-instrumental way. The poem itself is 'the product of an event of attention – the writer's attention to the world and language'. Attention produces poems, and poems become the object of readerly attention. There is a sense in which attention is so fundamental to poetry and indeed to our entire lives that its articulation as theory of poetics runs the risk of stating the obvious and the book becoming a a Casaubonesque 'Key to All Forms of Critical Reception'. Such transhistorical sweep is bound to be regarded as suspect, and therefore to put pressure on Alford's scholarship.

She speaks of tracing attention 'within as far-reaching an archive of poetic examples as my linguistic capabilities allow' and even 'slightly beyond'. That is an impressive range; she has added some Arabic to her knowledge of European languages and I'm deeply sympathetic to her ambition. It does, however, make huge linguistic and proof-reading demands, not all of which have been met. The first poem in her archive is Sappho Fragment 31, *Phainetai moi kenos isos theoisin*, but the Greek text printed alongside Anne Carson's translation is not the one that Carson gives in *If Not, Winter*, being one word different in the opening line of stanza 3 (*akēn* replaces the tmesis of *kat-agnumi*). Discussing Benn's 'Astern', Alford refers to the 'hesitancy of 'anhelden'', but there is no such verb in the poem, if indeed in German. Latin texts are sometimes slightly garbled (83, 217, 238, 299 n. 46). The translations of Petronius and Marcus Argentarius are given both in the text and in the notes. Alford refers to the 'indentations' in Oppen's 'Psalm' but the poem is printed without them. These are minor blemishes, which could be remedied in a second edition.

At this point, a reveal. I have known Alford for some years and am undeservedly name-checked in the acknowledgements. This links us back to the book's origins; what first caught my attention was her attempt to connect close reading with the kind of attention required to do duty to a person's human rights. This attempt has, rightly, I think, been abandoned. Reactions to poetry are too protean, as she says. The genocidal, I would argue, may be connoisseurs of their own poetry and regard its merits as demonstrating a racial superiority distinguishing them from their victims, whose culture they therefore seek to occlude. A Christian culture rooted not least in the Old Testament came to channel anti-Semitism, whose exterminatory mode blindly rejected the very notion of Jewish culture. The temptation – I would almost say the need – remains to assert that these are bad readers, but perhaps they are only partially blind. We might have to number Ezra Pound among them. In her 'Coda', Alford observes that 'Scholars of attention (poetic and otherwise) have jumped from the cultivation of attention to an assertion that cultivating attention leads necessarily to moral improvement'; at that point she parts ways, confining herself (minatory words in this context) to a 'more modest proposal', 'that poetic attention can cultivate the *necessary but insufficient grounds* for ethical response'. Perhaps we should be grateful that poetry cannot be thought, by itself, to control human behaviour for good or bad, though it can, perhaps, reinforce either tendency. The twin ethical goal of Alford's initial conception has therefore been abandoned, and this book marks the place that the study of attention has found in her intensive, expansive love of poetry. It's a rich haul.

Wild Homesickness

Romalyn Ante, *Antiemetic for Homesickness* (Chatto) £10
Rebecca Watts, *Red Gloves* (Carcanet) £9.99
Reviewed by Yvonne Reddick

Antiemetic for Homesickness (Chatto, 2020) and *Red Gloves* (Carcanet, 2020) gain a topical urgency in our age of pandemic and climate breakdown. Romalyn Ante's book was published during full lockdown, a debut that commands attention by evoking the NHS front line. Its author 'works as a registered nurse and psychotherapist,' the back cover

tells us, and Ante's poems provide a fascinating window into the lives of diaspora nurses.

Ante combines medical terminology with images of fruit, blossoms and bodies, creating characteristically original metaphors: 'amongst the haematoma of flowers'. From the first poem, specialist terms such as 'anti-emetic' and 'prophylaxis' rub shoulders with the *kamote* (sweet potato) and *kangkong* (water spinach) of Filipino gardens and cuisine. 'Names,' which won Poetry London's Clore Prize, has a shifting poetic form to mirror the travels of a family scattered between the Philippines, Britain and Oman: 'Riverside. Manila. London. Kurba'. Survival, endurance and healing are crucial foci – 'And the strongest part of me/ is the scar I hide underneath my fringe'. Ante joins Ocean Vuong in echoing Frank O'Hara, but her influences are global. References to Yi Yang-Yong appear alongside Filipino songs, *gunita* script, and nods to Neruda.

The book is steeped in 'The sanctity of blood', a turn of phrase encapsulating family relations, the healing arts, and the blood of suffering. We are introduced to a grandfather who was a shaman, to the vibrant traditions of the dance festival, and the fabled *nun*. A mother who has to leave her children to fly abroad is visualised as the *manananggal*, a woman who transforms into a winged monster: 'Aren't women more beautiful / when they scab into beasts?'.

Yet racism is an ever-present scourge in these poems. 'Nature Morte aux Tulipes' mourns the murdered overseas Filipino worker Joanna Demafelis, and elegises 'every exile-by-employment whose leaving poses great risks to their lives'. The book takes aim at British xenophobia after Brexit: we see a red Brexit battle-bus and hear the words of a colleague who says, '*Shall we shorten your name on your nametag/ so it's easier to remember?*'. Migrant nurses are celebrated as 'goddesses of caring and tending' at a time when austerity and the Covid-19 crisis are putting medical professionals under intense strain.

Rebecca Watts's *Red Gloves* takes a fresh look at nature red in tooth and claw. The book evokes environmental problems and connections between people and landscape with wonder, intellectual verve and wry humour. It expands the project Watts began in her debut *The Met Office Advises Caution* (2016). The poems explore the intricate links between human beings, landscape, animals, and the menace of climate change. Yet Watts also takes a humorously searching look at the literary canon, and at gender and power.

The book opens with 'Economics,' whose speaker lists connections to animals and plants. These range from an auspicious 'compact of magpies' to innumerable dandelion clocks. The poem ends with lyric wit and a skilfully-managed shift in tone:

You asked me would I move to the city to be with you.
I'm telling you what I saw; you can do the maths.

The speaker resists pressure to move away from her encounters with vibrant riverside ecosystems and, in the context of the rest of the collection, this has gendered as well as environmental aspects.

Human beings and their environment are presented as

intertwined. The tide flows into 'Amnesiac,' in which the North Sea is both 'anchoring' and 'slipping' – all anchor-points unstable in our age of climate change. 'Amnesiac' leads to the humorous 'Having Bled on a Library Book,' which meditates on the body's materiality and its 'seepage'. 'Admission' comes after several poems set in Cambridge's Addenbrookes Hospital, stressing the 'breaching' and 'Liquidation' of the body.

Cambridge's libraries, archives and waterways are beautifully sketched in the poems. Anyone who knows the city will recognise Watts's characters: students poring over computer screens, professors walking their dogs in the water-meadows. Low-lying and flood-prone, Cambridgeshire is an excellent location for exploring climate change. Jokes about climate breakdown are usually pretty bleak, yet Watts's local glimpses of a planetary problem have a witty freshness, as in 'Salvation':

Isn't it glorious! said Maria
when I caught up with her beside the river
on a 15°C December morning
in brilliant sunshine.

Let's enjoy it!
Before the water's risen to our knees
the Dutch will have invented
something wonderful.

From Fenland drainage to contemporary coastlines menaced by climate change, Watts wryly explores humankind's attempts to keep the waters at bay. In one poem about the rising seas, the sea

Recarpets
the carpet (water
and weed).

As the ice caps melt, we might as well swim rather than sinking. Watt's book celebrates the chilly thrills of wild swimming as an elemental way to immerse oneself in nature and come to terms with future deluges. *Red Gloves* joins Roger Deakin's *Waterlog* (1999) and Elizabeth Jane Burnett's *Swims* (2017) in a celebration of watery connections. Many of the localities are British rivers and lakes, although one poem takes us farther afield – 'Gloucester, Massachusetts' revisits the coastline of Lowell's Quaker graves, Bishop's fishhouses and Plath's beautiful Nauset for a time of rising seas:

black is the submarine's domain
from which no fishing boat

is coming back.

Shifting lines capture a bracing dip in Wordsworth's Grasmere, while bikini-clad women experience the 'deep chill' of Forces Falls. Danger lurks everywhere on the Cobb: 'Where the land drops off, disaster lies'. At all points, the shock of hitting water is a metaphor for the power of climate change.

One of the strongest poems is 'The Desire Path,' which evokes 'new twigs I'd thought of as budding/ bobbled

with disease' and 'the scattering of a few feathers/ like a planned demolition,' a refreshing antidote to the pastoral. 'The Entangled Bank,' which references Darwin, evokes 'innovations/ methods for survival', suggesting continuity in spite of threats. Interlocking sequences about gender, bird life, wild swimming and painting cross-reference each other thematically.

Pandemic, diaspora and climate change are such enormous issues that they might risk overwhelming the poems (and the reader). But Ante and Watts tackle them with enough personal anecdotes and humour to create compelling poetry.

Open your mouth

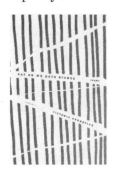

Eat Or We Both Starve, Victoria Kennefick (Carcanet)
£10.99
Reviewed by Kate Caoimhe Arthur

Compulsion, necessity, devotion, pleasure. In Victoria Kennefick's already lauded and reprinted debut our relationship with eating is not only relished but licked, smeared or rejected. And as readers, as the title of the book indicates, we are not observers of the feast but partakers.

Kennefick draws our eye and taste buds to the transformations of food. In 'Á La Carte' the steak 'pulsates'. In '(M)Eat' the creaturely nature of the 'muscle' hidden by the mother on the plate transforms the body of the child refusing it: 'Teeth turned to glass and shattered / in my mouth. All I could taste was blood.' In 'Second Communion' the child is revolted by the idea of eating a body in the act of Communion, in a sort of endless cycle of cannibalism: she asks, 'if I eat Jesus will he want to eat me?' In 'Learning to Eat my Mother, Where my Mother is the Teacher' she actually does cannibalise her mother, an act which is revenged in 'Choke' which imagines

my mother's finger
down my throat,
pushing
sugar
deep into me.

Kennefick's skill is in luring us in with the sensuousness of compulsion before turning our stomachs, as we see in 'Open Your Mouth' where the mother of Krishna is imagined falling through the vortex of his clay-eating mouth 'and within / that mouth/ another / universe' in free-falling endlessness.

There is so much to chew over and admire in this collection, but I particularly relished the Hunger Strike sequence. As a northerner, I was expecting a series entitled 'Hunger Strike' to reference the events that were a defining point of the eighties in this part of the world, but up here we have a tendency to think everything is about us. It is rather a reference to Susie Orbach's book about anorexia as a metaphor, and the strength of this group of poems is in their depiction of control of eating as a spiritual metaphor being overwhelmed by its bodily meaning. This group of poems, dotted throughout the collection, take in turn a female saint whose godliness was characterised by what she ingested or rejected. For Catherine of Siena it was vomiting sticks and 'kiss[ing] His holy prepuce' [foreskin], for Angela of Foligno consuming pus, scabs and lice are her path to sainthood, Veronica Guiliani licks skin and hair off the walls and floor 'My throat became thick with cobwebs'. The sequence concludes with 'Victoria Kennefick', who has absorbed the lessons from the saints to 'punch her stomach loose' and wish she could 'strip her bones' back to the essential. This poem vacillates between competing strong desires, to reduce to the bare bones, or to 'feast' as invited by the sacramental voice at the ends of the poem.

This tension is at the heart of the concerns of the collection, and of Kennefick's poetic aesthetic, swerving as it does from a sensual baroque excess, to steely Plathian precision. As it says in the fourth footnote to 'Hunger Strikes Gemma Galgani (1878–1903)' 'Am I threatened by flesh or its opposite?'

In the long poem 'Second Family' the complications and anxieties of family life, particularly in reference to step-families, is rendered in a cautious, tender exposure, which manages to be striking and intimate while holding its participants with love. The most vivid of these examinations, in the 'Extension' section, is of the poet's sister, who accompanies her through this sequence and throughout the collection, the young girl who 'padded through / the extension's freshly poured concrete in new summer sandals....your creamy contentment at reaching the centre' until she is rescued by the mother 'as you set in concrete'. This image of the child slowly becoming part of the house, and thereby becoming trapped, leaving her shoes behind as she is rescued, vivifies the statement at the heart of the poem 'Sister and me: / an infestation. We eat everything like moths...munching through memories'.

The sister also turns up in 'Forty Days' in which the Catholic practice of fasting and feasting is rendered in its most visceral way. Kennefick describes the approval they receive for their 'ecstasy of denial' in Lent, before it flicks suddenly and queasily to excess 'Resurrection with chocolate sauce made us sick'. Catholic Ireland is still coming to terms with its own excess and what it does with the bodies which it alternately controls, denies and overwhelms, but Kennefick clearly identifies and dramatizes the contradictory meanings of consumption. *Eat or we Both Starve* picks at the living history of the body in an Ireland and – from a legacy of famine, piety and misogyny –derives its own clear and identifiable note.

Small Incidents

Ian Seed, *The Underground Cabaret;* Harry Guest, *Last Harvest*; Michael Haslam, *Ickerbrow Trig*; Douglas Oliver, *Islands of Voices: Selected Poems* (ed. Ian Brinton)
Shearsman Books, £various
Reviewed by Ian Pople

There is something sad and premonitory about a book that calls itself, *Last Harvest.* And it is sad, too, that this book comes from someone as fine and underrated as Harry Guest, a poet who has existed under the radar for too long. *Last Harvest* contains poems that confirm Guest's virtues, a keen eye and a sense of the form of a poem. Guest's poems have always felt solid and well built, even where they nudge language and take where it might not always want to go. With that, too, is Guest's voice which, for someone associated with the avant-garde, is always conversational and warm. That voice has never been afraid to comment. And this last harvest contains writing which is possibly more opinionated that Guest's previous books.

One way in which these things move together is in the travel poems of which there are a number of good examples in *Late Harvest.* In 'Stone Islands', Guest writes, 'At the parched mouth / above some curling waves storm-petrels whirr / outside this so-called grotto. One huge leg / of limestone stamped in to these hardly ever tides / to cause a cave never inhabited / like elsewhere long ago, a given space / of ecstasy, blue mirror shimmering for / a beckoning sun.' Guest has a way of evoking the place with deft strokes and then opening it out to history with comments like 'never inhabited / like elsewhere long ago.' It's a pity then, that the book ends with a group of philippics that attack easy, contemporary targets such as art, poetry and education and their gate-keepers, 'critics' (Guest's inverted commas) and teachers ('sadly un-/der educated') and 'those cardboard cut-outs dubbed / 'celebrities''.

Ian Seed's *The Underground Cabaret* is a series of sophisticated prose poems. The poems often give a surreal, dream-like picture of small incidents in charged, mysterious contexts. They are written with an easy elegance which underpins the surrealism and draws the reader into a world which feels real and whole, somehow. One of the blurb comments suggests that these pieces are actually about 'what it means to be human', and there is a lot of truth in that. In part, that sense is a result of Seed's skill as a writer, in part too, it is the element of embedded realism which gives the pieces their foundation; an air of normalcy that runs through even the 'weirdest' of the pieces.

This is the whole of 'Morning After': 'I wake to find the house has fallen apart. I'm lying in bed exposed to the street. 'What happened?' I shout to my wife. She is sitting on the toilet, in the fresh air, laughing.' The first sentence is carefully bathetic, a feeling that is emphasised by the depiction of the wife, 'in the fresh air.' It is these quiet details that add solidity to the piece; along with the use of the present tense which creates a factual feel about the text.

Michael Haslam has always been a practitioner of an aurally dense poetry. The voice almost harks back to the alliterative verse of Old and Middle English, and the sound world is rhythmic and pulsed. With that commitment to aural density is an equal commitment to the landscape of the Calder Valley in which Haslam has lived since 1970. That is not the only landscape present in Haslam's new book, *Ickerbrow Trig*. He also writes about the Bolton area of his childhood. Although Haslam writes that he does not believe in fairies or sprites, he does believe in their being 'prime elements of the human imagination'. Here he adduces Roger Langley's 'Jack' as 'a common spirit, beyond belief', or as Haslam puts it for himself, 'the tail-end of spirit, and two thirds of wit,' his 'irresponsible imp.' That impishness means that Haslam's poetry has, in all its density, a leavening sense of humour. Although Haslam's 'I' is clearly the authorising consciousness of the poems, the seriousness he takes himself is never overwhelming. However, Haslam has a serious eye which takes in with considerable precision the industrial archaeology of his area; 'A shell / of stone gathers its moss. A sunk tank fills with sediment, with alder, / kingcup, saxifrage, a picturesque of heritage of the industrial age / and locus for some psychic delectation, snap for a repast / with ghosts of workers clogging up the path back from the past.'

Douglas Oliver's *Islands of Voices: Selected Poems* reprints a selection of poems from Oliver's multifarious and now fugitive earlier collections. Oliver was often bracketed with the Cambridge poets, and J.H.Prynne is quoted in the introduction as commenting that 'this whole achievement is quite overwhelming.' In contrast to many of that grouping, Oliver's poetry was often, if not mostly, socially and politically committed. An early major poem, 'The Infant and the Pearl' was a damning critique of both Thatcherism and the failure of the Labour governments of the seventies to address the social issues of the time. Oliver's sense of commitment was also clearly affected by the death in 1969 of his infant son, Tom, who was born with Down's Syndrome. The sequence 'An Island that is All the World', which is excerpted here, contains poems that portray with considerable empathy lives lived in the shadow of loss and exile. 'The Ferry Pirate' describes one of Oliver's trips back and forth over the Channel, 'That sea is always fairly near / under the rails of night ferries / swaying with unsteady thoughts, blackening in crisis, / roughening with time or fortune, drawn on /by inkless nibs.' Oliver's gift in these poems is to adroitly recreate the atmosphere of a place and time and to pan out from it to the emotions imbued in that atmosphere. Over the whole course of his writing career, Oliver had that knack of keeping the reader equally aware of place and time and atmosphere; for all their commit-

ment, these poems are very sensual and visual.

This volume is a slightly frustrating selection. It is a cliché to lament the exclusion of poems that one has particularly cherished from individual books. However, Oliver's achievement was such that lament is inevitable. Oliver's texts were often a mingling of poetry and prose that refracted of each other. Part of that achievement is contained here, but some is lost.

Consciously Awkward

Rebecca Perry, *Stone Fruit* (Bloodaxe) £10.99
Reviewed by Genevieve Stevens

Where *Beauty/Beauty*, Perry's previous collection conjured Sasquatch, Stegosaurus and a million silver spiders for company, *Stone Fruit* occupies the psychic territory of in-betweenness and memory. In the first of its three sections, 'beaches', a sequence of fourteen poems emerges from the shoreline as their narrator wanders the beach with sympathetic curiosity, stuck in the interstitial space between a closed-off past and an uncertain future. It's a place thick with questions about the natural world, frequently projecting back onto the human body observing it: 'will the crab come back out of the same hole / when the sea retreats // is it a man or a body'. Convictions too, if they are asserted, are soon overturned or pushed to absurdity: 'there are things / you can say absolutely / a man should not be able to bear the weight / of a refuse truck on his chest, begins 'beaches (8)'

With the exception of 'beaches (1)', this sequence is written in lower case and without punctuation. The impression is of a tidal song, a meditation on the sea and sea changes in the speaker's life, each poem washing up flotsam of hearsay, scraps of memory, half-formed questions. Though an effective technique to heighten the poem's sense of immediacy, of things being worked out, unobstructed, on the page, it's hard to sustain over thirteen poems. By 'beaches (5)' I found myself longing for breath, emphasis, a gear-shift, just a solitary full stop. The risk in making everything uniformly fluid is that pretty soon, nothing is – what initially feels free and impressionistic begins to sound one-note. 'beaches (10)' does something different and is mightier for it. Here, Perry uses spacing in the line to create not only breath, but a clear and measured sense of the speaker's uncertainty:

what am I trying to say
fear seems heavier in winter
  in my hard room
  as the swans separate

and the snow comes down

In the four stand-alone poems that make up the middle section, Perry often retreats into description at the expense of music and vitality. Consider this excerpt from 'The execution was conducted in the open air':

I walked into the park after the blizzard.
The air had the muffled quality that follows snowfall.

No distinction could be made between the whites slopes of the park and the bright grey sky. 'The ducks in the pond tipped back and forth.' These observations, detached and measured as they are, effectively have the poem by the throat. I longed for a sudden swerve, a kick back or lurch of perspective. Perry instead reflects, 'To paint the white of snow is only to capture the light that falls on it, as with all things', which is interesting but not strong enough to lift the rest of the poem up and out of itself. 'Apples are 1/4 air', the final poem in this section, gets the closest; punctuation, spacing, disrupted syntax are all in full swing and so the poem is able to travel and swerve:

In the greenhouse he is so far away
like a man underwater, a man in a block of ice. When I dream, his mouth

becomes a pea-sized hole and I press the tip of my little finger to it.
I eat him whole.

This is Perry at her best, operating at the limits of her control, engaging her reader to share in (rather than state) one of her principal preoccupations: the mutability of the physical form.

Such transformative zeal does not carry over into the final section, an extended lyrical poem about competitive trampolining. Although informative and often shocking, particularly with regards to the vulnerability and suffering of young female competitors, the poetry does little to enact the twists and turns of its subject. Perhaps the obligations of memory suppress the impulse to make things strange. For example, one girl is under so much pressure that she has 'ceased to have periods', but then Perry over-explains cause and effect, 'she had been pushed too far'. I found myself wishing Perry had used more of the highly specialised language of the sport and baffled us with its unfamiliar music, or that she had taken one of her evocative brief descriptions: 'dim beige halls', 'bottles of frozen orange squash' and grown the poem from that point, or played with the idea that she touches on in the key line 'I landed in the vast / safe space between total failure / and absolute perfection'.

The shape of the collection is a puzzle. Perhaps the four middle poems are the 'stone' to the surrounding fruit of 'beaches' and 'On trampolining'? Or you could argue that the theme of memory – all its complicated and unreliable machinery – binds the three parts together: but couldn't that be said of everything? 'To explain anything', art critic Adrian Stokes wrote, 'we go back.' Structure aside, *Stone Fruit* seems too bound by the parameters Perry has

set herself to be as brilliantly strange and fresh as *Beauty/Beauty*. There are moments of flight in *Stone Fruit*, but its consciously awkward routine inhibits the full range of her proven capacity.

Moladh Garry MacKenzie

Garry MacKenzie, *Ben Dorain: A Conversation with a Mountain* (Irish Pages Press) £20
Reviewed by Andrew McNeillie

Garry MacKenzie's refreshingly original *Ben Dorain* can only summon before us the shade of Dhonnchaidh Bhain, as he was in Gaelic, known otherwise as Duncan Bàn MacIntyre. MacIntyre has long been celebrated in Scotland (but never enough) for his songs, and above all the virtuosic 'Moladh Beinn Dobhrain' – 'Praise of Ben Dorain', an intricately figured work of intensely visualised detail, composed 'To the tune of a Pibroch' – literally 'pipe music' – atonal bagpipe music, known as 'ceol mor', 'big music'.

'Moladh Beinn Dobhrain' is all the more astonishing in being in its making a 500 line-plus feat of memory by a man who could neither read nor write. The situation is Homeric and the highly mellifluous song itself classical and impersonal, yet expressive of intense passion. John Tonge in his landmark study *The Arts of Scotland* (1938), referring to the absence of the humanist element in Celtic visual art, suggested that its 'filigree technique' characterises the 'consummate and intricate... art-music' of the pibroch. That amounts to saying that Celtic oral, visual, and musical culture enjoyed common forms of coherence. As we stalk the poet through his poem, the assymetries of a pibroch mark our step, switching from 'urlar' (theme) to 'siubhal' (variation) and in this case 'an crundludh' (finale), preceded by again an 'urlar'. I believe this is about as echt as it gets.

The key period in Bàn MacIntyre's life of present interest was passed as a forester in the service of the Earl of Breadalbane, in Coire-Cheataich, and Benn-Dourainn, Argyllshire. That work involved the stalking and shooting of deer. This interaction, this dance of death, between man and deer, with his rifle between them both, is at the heart of the poem. Another of his poems 'Song to a Gun Named Nic Coisem' extends our understanding of the relationship. Daily and seasonal exposure to the terrain of Ben Dorain made an acute and sensitive naturalist of the poet. We should beware being presentists and calling him even so much as a proto-ecologist. It is surely tempting, though, as it is with John Clare.

To aspire to follow anywhere near his footsteps is a

courageous thing. But this in his fashion is what Garry MacKenzie has done in a highly innovative, ecologically aware way, in territory he too knows intimately and belongs in, though not with rifle in hand. He stalks poetry instead. Together they dance a dance not of death but of life. We may burden the exercise with environmental politics if we wish, but that would be a mistake, as Kathleen Jamie makes clear in her note on the poem. The poem is that rare thing these days, a celebration of the wild in and for itself. His bagpipe music is as much visual as aural, and plainsong more the character of his speech. The poem has Poundian resonance and Mallarméan throws of the dice. It plays with 'adjacencies', on a principle attributed to Jorie Graham. There are passages of text running parallel, and one or two side glosses, refencing sources as diverse as Darwin and T.H. Clutton-Brock. So it is a poem for eye and ear, with many moments that capture exquisitely the terrain, and the 'Deer on the High Hills' in Iain Crichton-Smith's formulation in all their magic. Wallace Stevens gave us thirteen ways of looking at a blackbird. Garry MacKenzie discovers as many and more ways of not only looking at but seeing, and seeing into, the Ben Dorain of today, and its hinds and stags. Irish Pages Press will find it hard to follow this fine book with anything half as good, but let's hope they will succeed, for here too is not only a new poet to most of us, but a new imprint. They couldn't be worthier of each other. The two enjoy uncommon forms of coherence.

Double Dose

Christopher Meredith, *Still* ; *Please* (Seren) both £9.99
Reviewed by Sam Adams

Christopher Meredith has long enjoyed a high reputation as poet and writer of prose fiction. This is still a remarkable event: the joint publication of a novella and a new collection of poems.

The contents of *Still,* gathered over several years, are presented in four sections, the last, the only one bearing its own title, 'Still air', being the poet's share of a joint publication with artist and print-maker Sara Philpott in 2016.

Meredith is Welsh speaking. In the glossary of places mentioned in the collection, the site of a former slate quarry near Blaenau Ffestiniog, its yawning depths now lake-filled, evokes a response in the old language, 'Dail poethion, Cwmorthin'. Although there are inevitable similarities, since the same scene, tall nettles growing by the

ruins of the former manager's house, is the subject of both, the accompanying English poem, 'Nettles, Cwmorthin' is not a translation. The demands of language and prosody in Welsh are different from those customary in English. Imagery is common to both, but the tradition of layering images, *dyfalu,* is typically Welsh. Hopkins' poetry shows its influence, and it is present in Meredith's 'Winter Woods', for example: where snowflakes, 'ice crystals finialled like/ the ideograms of stars … pattern the gravid void like/ free fallers clasping hands … to feather, copter,/ this gathering/ of crystal feathers,/ rock and float, slide, sideslip,/ tumble, float again/ ride down the zigzag/ seesaws of the half-sustaining air … they fall/ until at last they settle their wafer/ on the tongue of earth.' Another striking example is provided by tide-line 'Horseshoe Crabs'. Under 'planished clouds', they too are metal, 'heaped shields', 'slime lacquered bronzes … each disc a warrior forged'. There are poems to remind us how blessedly unreliable memory can sometimes be, while others are journal entries for days out in Llandudno where a swing band plays and, offshore, windfarms are 'milking small change from the fitful breeze/ as if a hundred clocks were running down'; or a walk in the Brecon Beacons, 'On Allt-yr-Esgair', where Roland Mathias trod before, to produce a small rhapsody on curvature on earth and in the stars, and 'Steampunk Jungle', which (if I am not much mistaken) records a visit to the site of the former Gleision Colliery, where the deaths of four men in the flooded mine are marked by an informal memorial. *Still* is a polished performance. The poet's keen eye and characteristically inventive response are the unifying features in an otherwise diverse collection. Precise observation of subjects and events is one thing; finding, and blending, the precise words to convey the experience is entirely another. But this instinct Meredith possesses, whether he is teasing out the peculiarly static nature of personal recollection, or descanting on evanescence in the movement of snow.

Please is a literary high wire act, a novella whose autodidact narrator's preferred reading is 'reference books and dictionaries'. Vernon is packed to bursting with words and self-acknowledged 'affected pomposity'. He is proud of his linguistic excesses, producing puns and word associations like a prestidigitator rabbits from a hat with a self-congratulatory '(ha!!)'.We are regularly reminded that he is profusely verbose not in the written word alone, as the text testifies, but also in his diligently acquired oral prolixity. He hears himself 'drone'. Briefly, he is a bore. Nevertheless, he rises from humble clerk to a senior position in 'human resources', one of a number of aspects of our daily intercourse with others satirised in the text.

The action revolves around Hannah, whose teacher training studies have been interrupted by an unplanned pregnancy and consequent marriage to Derek. As an assistant in the local Co-op shoe department she kneels before Vernon and he is smitten. It is her inflected 'Please', with its burden of meaning that gives the book its title. They are well-matched. Local opinion, voiced in the vernacular, is that 'She's a dog, mun. Plain as a pikelet', while he is 'an insignificant little squit'.

The highlights are her two adulterous episodes, the first with the narrator, who duly replaces the summarily dismissed Derek, the second (as chance would have it, observed by the narrator) with a hirsute educational adviser. Much later, there is a curious case of accidental murder at sea, albeit fantasised, Vernon's furious response to Hannah's imputation that the elaborate scaffolding of his learning is founded on initial failure of the 11+.

Old and widowed, returned to the honeymoon island of his ardent young manhood, Vernon chances to meet at the bar another traveller in reminiscent mood, a grossly fat retired academic with interests very like his own, and another windbag to boot, who slips confidentially into the familiar Valley's demotic. Which of the other two men in Hannah's life does he turn out to be?

Please is a high-wire act and a tour-de-force, and withal, incisively human and mordantly humorous, of a piece with the narrator's insistent voice.

The Sea of a Single Day

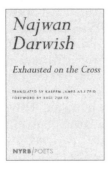

Najwan Darwish, *Exhausted on the Cross,* translated by Kareem James Abu-Zeid (NYRB Poets) $16.99
Choi Seungja, *Phone Bells Keep Ringing for Me*, translated by Won-Chung Kim and Cathy Park Hong (Action Books) US $18.00
Reviewed by Evan Jones

The title of Palestinian poet Najwan Darwish's *Exhausted on the Cross* sets the tone for poems of despair and resistance. Darwish's voice is often plural, not a speaking for but a speaking to. The title poem opens, 'The ones hanging / are tired, / so bring us down / and give us some rest.' It's enough now, the suffering and occupation of so many lifetimes. Yet Darwish's poems don't let up or give in: 'I'm not King David – / I won't sit at the gate of regret / and sing you psalms of lamentation / after the sins.' What we read instead is sadness, a consideration of loss and its weight on the living.

'They Woke You at Dawn' is dedicated to Rasmea Odeh, a convicted terrorist or a great hero, depending. Her complicated life (Odeh maintains her conviction is based on a confession she gave under torture) is portrayed compassionately by the poet:

> Christ was a *fedayee,* just like you,
> but he was condemned and crucified
> in the sea of a single day, while you –
> your cross is raised with every dawn.

'*Fedayee*', the translator tells us, is 'an Arabic word that denotes both guerilla-style resistance and the sacrificing of one's own life'. In this short poem, Darwish exemplifies Odeh in her prison of living history, a martyr whose every day is suffering.

The representation of history is prominent in the book. 'A Story from Shiraz,' begins, 'Read history, but don't believe the historians'. The prose 'story' retells an anecdote of the meeting of Tamerlane – the Timurid conqueror, subject of a poem by Edgar Allan Poe – and the great poet Hafez al-Shirazi. In a ghazal, Hafez had written that he would surrender Bukhara and Samarkand for the hand of an attractive Turk. Tamerlane has taken offence to this, two of his most prized cities. Yet Hafez, in his impoverished state, clothes dishevelled, someone who should be unnerved before a tyrant, speaks instead like 'a kindly old schoolmaster who feels for an unruly child'. And the poet continues: 'It's with his words that we face the invaders now, the ones who, surprised at our own extravagance, keep asking the same question: 'You're still resisting, in such a wretched state?'' The metaphor holds – and is past and present in Darwish's poems.

In his afterword, translator Kareem James Abu-Zeid highlights Darwish's 'skillful manipulation of the various registers of the Arabic language, from classical idioms to regional expressions in different dialects'. This change in register isn't always apparent in the English translations, and Abu-Zeid's language can be wordy. There is a slim UK edition of Darwish's poems, *Embrace,* co-translated by Atef Alshaer and Paul Batchelor, where the language is sharper.

There have been a small number of significant and revelatory translations and publications of South Korean and diaspora poets in the past while – recent works by Don Mee Choi, Cathy Park Hong (one of the co-translators of this book), Yi Sang and Monica Youn come to mind. Selected from Choi Seungja's five collections and arranged in five sections, *Phone Bells Keep Ringing for Me* begins in the visceral body and progresses towards a larger cultural critique. Her poems are illuminating and focus on a worldview different from the work of contemporary Western writers. Seungja's chief theme is the valuelessness of poetry in the modern world – prescribed via the metaphor of a woman's life. The sequence 'Not Forgetting or Memorandum' identifies the significance of this lack in culture, even as it revels in the connections, especially in part 10: 'And I want to make a final decision / whether I will kiss your face / or / smear shit on your face.' This quick switch between the sentimental and excremental is one of Seungja's strengths, and the reader never quite knows where one of her poems might wind up. In 'The Tribe of Capital', she goes further:

> In this world (covered by the tribe of capital)
> where money mothers give birth to money babies
> and capital mothers, capital babies,
> I will raise capital kids into mothers,
> if the baby of the baby of the baby of capital can be a poem
> (all poets, lie prostrate).

For Seungja, the value of life *can* lead to poetry, the highest and most significant output – even as poetry is supposedly prostrate before the building of capital. The terminology is dehumanizing but has an end outside of the culture of money-making, developed within the intelligence and wit of Seungja's thinking. 'The Tribe of Capital' calls out finally, bracketed, separate: '(Teach me a postmodern way; / I don't know why I can only talk in this traditional way.) There is a great loneliness in these poems, a sometimes-clinical assessment and evaluation of the world, but also charm and curiosity.

Park Hong, in her introduction, positions Seungja's historical and thematic concerns, but doesn't really explain the formal elements of her writing in the Korean language, so it's hard to have a sense of what Seungja should sound like in English. The translations are dry, mostly, statement-like, with some anaphora. And the language occasionally falls into cliché: 'On Woman' begins, 'Every woman has a grave inside / where death and birth sweat it out.' The poem develops from there into a painful metaphor for motherhood, but that 'sweat it out' drags the initial image to the gym and doesn't bond with the rest.

A Disarray of Stuff

Yeow Kai Chai, *One to the Dark Tower Comes*
(Firstfruits Publications) £19.50
Reviewed by Jee Leong Koh

What do you get if you transpose John Ashbery and John Yau into the equatorial register of Singapore? You get Yeow Kai Chai. Yeow stands out in his generation of poets for not having gone to Oxford or Cambridge, but studying locally. Unlike the next generation who found their way to Harvard, Columbia, and Brown, he absorbed his American influences from afar. These influences arrived via poetry, but also pop culture, especially computer games, film, and music. He wrote about the last for local magazines; was, in fact, the editor-in-chief of *My Paper*, a daily given out free at train stations, bus interchanges, and office complexes.

The title of his third collection *One to the Dark Tower Comes* is taken from mad Edgar in *King Lear*, via Robert Browning, we may think. Words of disguise then, but also alarmingly close to death. However, the epigraph directs us to a different source: Stephen King's *The Dark Tower Series*, which melds together elements of dark fantasy, science fiction, horror, and Western. Its hero, Roland Deschain of Gilead, speaks for Yeow in his bleak finality, 'We spread the time as we can, but in the end the world takes it all back.'

One to the Dark Tower Comes is shadowed everywhere by death, but the surprise is that death is not treated with any of the familiar attitudes. Instead, the dominant tone is one of playfulness, in places insouciance. Death is confronted with a spread of ideas, an exhibit of observations, a gauntlet of music.

> Like I said,
> there's a certain charm
> about a disarray of stuff
> lying around for the hell of it:
> mini-muffins, bad coffee,
> assorted bagatelles...
> (from 'Angel Lust')

The speaker may zoom in on a fly, but he is constantly aware that 'a flick of a dimmer' may lose, or suggest, everything. The poetry thus embraces the tentative and disorderly plenitude of the world. We see in it the Ashberyian interest in clichés, the Rabelaisian delight in wordplay, the fracture of standardized language, the parade of fantastical personages such as the Absent Conductor, the Handyman, the One True Valentine, the Sweet Madrigalist, the Axletree, all wearing their secret identities like superhero costumes or supermodel couture.

> So, here we are, strutting across the runway,
> Oftentimes bulimic and inconsolable,
> Trying on the vendibles for size and weight.
> Shoulder blades jut out through cotton.
> (from 'Another to the Dark Tower Comes')

From embracing everything, excluding nothing, comes a deep compassion for the suffering that we put ourselves through, imaginary or otherwise. Seen from the telescope end of death, the only thing that comes sharply into view is charity.

Seeing is very much the task in *One to the Dark Tower Comes*. There are ekphrastic poems here looking at 'The Laughing Cavalier' by Frans Hals and photographs of Slunkariki, a hut by Icelandic artist Solon Gudmundsson. The most striking aspect of these poems is their concern not just with what they see, but how they see, and how they describe the experience of seeing. Looking at the Rolfsaker Man, a 4,500-year-old skeleton perfectly preserved by the lime secretions of oysters, the poet asks about the adequacy of journalism – 'Do the sands add up? Does this fulfil the four Ws and one H?' – and dismisses the authority of social science – 'Lose the key and the bleeding sociologist's argot.' – before settling for a sneaky snap that locks him into an existential identification with the long-dead man: 'All this while the dispassionate lens click into I, shutter clamping down like a crab to the end of time, or an enemy's lunch.'

The willful heterogeneity of Yeow's verse is unified formally by two series that weave through the collection, the first about space, the second about time. There are eight poems that all bear the same title of 'A Slit from Sternum to Pizzle' (I did not know before that a pizzle is the penis of a bull.) All eight poems have thirteen lines each. The scenes and characters keep changing, but consistently they have to do with difficult ascents – up an apartment block, Rapunzel's tower, perhaps the Empire State Building – and terrifying, but liberating, descents: 'All the amazing space opening up around you.'

The second series is framed as Quarterly Reports on various institutions, people, and objects. 'Quarterly Report No. 1' is on a city waste incinerator. 'Quarterly Report No. 4' is on a pachinko parlor vending machine. Whereas 'Quarterly Report No. 6' is on an ethnological warfare atrocity exhibition, 'Quarterly Report No. 9' is on a pack of drapery and roller-blind professionals. Borrowing the language of its chosen topics, this series achieves its most powerful effects when it mixes the bureaucratic and the bucolic, the modern and the mythical, as in the first Quarterly Report on an advanced water treatment plant, which begins in this way:

After all that's been said and done, that's always the unnameable sense of loss after The Flood, despite our historical efforts with the hacking, piping, re-tiling and varnishing.

One to the Dark Tower Comes arrives fourteen years after Yeow's last collection. (That book *Pretend I'm Not Here* is also, in my opinion, a masterpiece.) The long interval has more to do with the publisher than the writer, but the publication itself is also well worth waiting for – it is a thing of beauty. In addition to the striking typographical designs inside the book, the black-and-white cover sleeve may be removed and unfolded into an eye-catching poster in landscape format.

Pandemix

Michèle Roberts, *Quarantine* (Melos Press) £5
Paul O'Prey, *Fleet* (Melos Press) £5
Kat Payne Ware, *The Live Album* (Broken Sleep) £6.50
Briony Collins, *Blame it on Me* (Broken Sleep) £6.50
Reviewed by Rory Waterman

Several editors have grumbled to me over the past year and a half about the proliferation of Covid poems. A million poets, it seemed, sat to write about the first lockdown as it happened, and Michèle Roberts was one of them. Back then, and though I expected them to try, I wondered whether poets would have much to say: pandemics, especially when they seem to have a fairly comparable likelihood of affecting anyone, rarely prove fertile ground for poetry. Spanish flu probably killed more people than the Great War that preceded it; find me an anthology of Spanish flu poems.

Roberts succeeds through a blend of subjectivity and objectivity, as well as brevity and precision – or rather

through idiosyncrasy coupled with a knack of memorably giving voice to things so many of us shared. She almost makes me nostalgic. Against a backdrop of restrictions – 'government ads / barking Stay at Home', leaning 'on my area of railings' – we are presented with the small world effect of lockdown, the sudden and otherwise glorious British spring of 2020 during which 'the clematis hurtles / – a blooming miracle – / out of the rosebush' and petals 'open like hands / defenceless, generous', the street that 'empty of traffic / turns inside out / becomes our meeting-room', the lucid dreams so many people have reported. The following incongruous lines surprised me rather until I realised they belonged in that context:

Already I've watched my dentist
 – rugby player in cool blue scrubs –
hurl himself face down
on his spreadeagled naked date
tongue her cunt enthusiastically.

Any poet can have us nod in full or partial recognition, of course: it is the easiest trick to master. But most of these seven poems are beguilingly multifaceted too. The finest is probably the opener, 'Enclosure', in which a

Honeypot garden
 – small walled plot –
sucks in insects. A
Cabbage White surveys choisya
blossom & a Red Admiral
hovers past, swerves
to the early roses.

The sudden little destabilising enjambments are perfect as the insects enter the stage. Overhead, there are 'police buzzy as flies / swivelling, spying'. On micro and macro levels, life comes in and out of view, albeit with different intentions. Only on the human, grounded level, the one we are stuck with, is there stasis.

Poets have always loved their rivers, and over the past couple of decades there has been a spate (pun intended) of long poems, pamphlets and collections travelling them, from Alice Oswald's *Dart* and *A Sleepwalk on the Severn* to Alan Baker's *Riverrun*, a sonnet sequence that bounds along part of the turgid Trent. Paul O'Prey's subject is the maligned River Fleet, Alexander Pope's 'king of dykes', which began as a spring-rich, widening stream, became Londinium's eastern border, was reduced to a fetid sewer in a growing London, and now runs almost entirely underground, emerging into the Thames through a concrete drainage outlet. Fittingly, then, this is a sequence in search of a river as much as about it, full of myth and history and a sense of time's convection current. At the source,

I cup my hands and press
into the wet turf

deep into the cold bog
weeping last year's rain

This is the only unadulterated river he finds, without drawing on other kinds of source, for soon 'the river is taken, / ushered through a dark and hidden cage'.

'The world is old, mad, blind and dying', he writes, slightly altering Shelley's description of King George III in 'England in 1819'. The appropriated line isn't Shelley's finest, though it partially makes up for that with revolutionary zeal fervent enough to have rendered the poem unpublishable in its time. O'Prey's sentiment is what one is supposed to say, and the anthropomorphisms don't quite work. But what saves this pamphlet from the pitfalls of obviousness are his frequently limpid descriptions and their juxtapositions:

> And yet, from this concrete dungeon
> comes the chatter of any river
> tripping on itself, urgent for the ocean,
> breaking and remaking
>
> singing as it starves
> like a thrush in winter.

For O'Prey, the modern Fleet is not just the conduit for effluent that it has become, but also a conduit for considering the earth's inexorable desire to undo our damage. At Thames Beach,

> The wind warm
> against my face,
> its salt on my tongue,
> whispers absolution.

Kat Payne Ware's debut, *The Live Album*, is a glorious oddity in two parts. In the first, different pork products jostle for our attention ('Carve me as a figurehead, baby', says the rib), or are farcically juxtaposed with epigraphs. 'Cheek' ('a versatile, flavoursome and cheap cut that deserves much more attention – Campbell's Prime Meat Ltd, *A-Z of Meat*') says:

> Let me turn the other
> for a little kiss.
> O to be underrated
> to shy from praise
> and to bruise slow
> in cheap cider
> and a low heat.

'Shoulder' ('the most forgiving cut on the animal – Kevin Gillespie, *Pure Pork Awesomeness*') informs us that 'On the internet you can read about / Ten Great Moments in Forgiveness History.'

The second section replaces seduction with reality, but remains ostensibly playful. It contains a forgettable erasure poem, and a butcher's diagram of a pig in which the names of cuts are replaced, apparently at random, with financial words: 'EQUITY', 'CAPITAL', 'PROFIT', and so on. But it also contains the pamphlet's real prize: coldly memorable, often somehow moving poems setting a main text against another in footnotes. In 'Scolding', 'When I'm ready, I'm submerged / and the priestly hands of the hoist / guide me through the long trough', says a pig. 'I become reflective // as a buffed nail, as a waxed / bikini line, as a waxing moon'. The footnotes, much longer than the poem itself, are lifted from the instructions for Frontamec's scalding tank and dehairing machine: 'In case of a new installation, the machine will traditionally be installed as a double dehairing machine with opposite rotation of each pig'; '*Be prepared for the unexpected* by stocking rubber fenders, drum bearings and paddles.' Payne Ware is a dexterous writer with a knack for keeping us interested, and her desire to eschew direct polemic, and lack of interest in demonstrating an unimpeachable morality – so common at present among poets drawn to writing about social issues – is refreshing. She leaves the thinking to us.

We are predisposed to human narratives, even if some poets pretend we aren't and some others dive too readily into narcissism or schmaltz. Briony Collins's *Blame it on Me* focuses on the inevitability, then aftermath, of the death of her mother, when the poet was a child: 'her son crying / because he didn't understand & / her daughter crying because she did'. The best poems in this pamphlet – and there are plenty of them – detail pellucid personal memories and remove the poet from focus, sometimes through use of the third person: 'Her husband's bed where he shapes / the duvet into her', and 'soaks up his permanent / night, buries himself in her pillow'. In other poems, she detaches herself from herself, and observes, layering adult experience on top of ruptured childhood innocence:

> I'm a single, solitary rock
> inbound for the sofa,
>
> which catches me in its
> cushions and cuddles me
>
> close to stop me shaking.
> I'm the most delicate comet,
>
> still learning to live
> with the trepidation
>
> of elegant flight.

The pamphlet then moves through family upheavals, to find the speaker marooned in young adulthood:

> There must be one thing – *one thing* –
> to get up for today
>   (*pick at that thought like a day-old scab,*
>   *tender and ripe for another blood-letting*).
>
> Who would notice if you stayed in bed
> and fantasised about dark passages,
> the damp earth, eulogies?

The effect is somewhat diluted by the length of the sequence. This is a long pamphlet, almost a collection, and several poems half-repeat others, apparently more by accident than design. Still, it is a bold and moving debut.

Some Contributors

Jee Leong Koh's latest book is a hybrid work of fiction, *Snow at 5 PM: Translations of an insignificant Japanese poet.* **Nell Prince** is a writer from Lincolnshire, has had poems published in *New Poetries VIII,* and is currently a subeditor at *Strandlines.* **Joyelle McSweeney** is the author of ten books of poetry, fiction, translation, essays, and plays, including, most recently, *Toxicon & Arachne* (Corsair Books, 2021) and *The Necropastoral: Poetry, Media, Occults,* a work of goth eco-criticism. She lives in the US and edits the international press, Action Books. **Olivia McCannon**'s *Exactly My Own Length* won the Fenton Aldeburgh Prize. Her long sequence, *The Archives of Z,* is forthcoming, and an 'Anthropocene' *Beauty and Beast,* with Clive-Hicks Jenkins, appears autumn/winter 2021 (Design for Today). **Damian Grant** taught literature for many years at the University of Manchester, publishing criticism on poets and novelists as well as occasional poems. He now lives (and continues to write) in retirement in France. **Rachel Spence** is a poet and arts journalist who divides her time between London, Ludlow and Venice. She has published two pamphlets *Furies* (Templar, 2016) and *Call and Response* (The Emma Press, 2020) and one collection *Bird of Sorrow* (Templar, 2018). She has two books forthcoming for 2022. *Art, Money and Power – A Toxic Triangle* (Hurst Publishing) and *On Cities: Venice* (The Ivory Press). **Christopher Riesco** lives and works in Manchester as an administrator in the education system. He is a graduate of the Writing School at Manchester Metropolitan University. A descendant of transatlantic antique dealers, he is interested in the English Metaphysical Poets and their Spanish equivalents and rivals. Poems appear, sometimes, somehow, in magazines, including *Bodega, Postcards from Malthusia* and the *Black Horse Review.* He writes reviews of poetry books at https://lordminimus.substack.com/. **Michelle Penn**'s pamphlet, *Self-portrait as a diviner, failing* (2018), won the Paper Swans Prize. She has published in journals worldwide and plans innovative poetry/art/music events in London as part of Corrupted Poetry. **Sarah White**'s seventh book, a lyric memoir, *The Poem Has Reasons: a story of far love,* is forthcoming from Dos Madres Press. **Sam Trainor** is originally from Birmingham. He is a senior lecturer in Translation Studies at the *Université de Lille* in the North of France. **Michael Edwards** is a poet in English and French, whose *At the Brasserie Lipp* was published by Carcanet in 2019. The first British member of the Académie française, he was knighted in 2014. **Caroline Clark**'s first collection is *Saying Yes In Russian* (Agenda Editions). Her second, *Sovetica,* is out now with CB editions. **Francesca Brooks** is a writer and researcher living in Manchester and working at the University of York. Her poetry was recently longlisted for *Primers 6* (Nine Arches Press) and has appeared in journals including *Lighthouse* and *Structo.* **Greg Thomas** is a writer based in Glasgow. He is the author of *Border Blurs: Concrete Poetry in England and Scotland* (Liverpool University Press, 2019). **Rachel Hadas**'s recent books (summer 2021) are *Love and Dread,* poetry, and *Piece by Piece,* prose. A new collection, *Pandemic Almanac,* is forthcoming in March 2022. **Judith Woolf** is a literary critic and translator, with special interests in 20th century Italian-Jewish writing and narrative patterns in European literature. She is an honorary fellow of the University of York.

Colophon

Editors
Michael Schmidt
John McAuliffe

Editorial Manager
Andrew Latimer

Contributing Editors
Vahni Capildeo
Sasha Dugdale
Will Harris

Design
by Andrew Latimer

Editorial address
The Editors at the address on the right. Manuscripts cannot be returned unless accompanied by a stamped addressed envelope or international reply coupon.

Trade distributors
NBN International

Represented by
Compass IPS Ltd

Copyright
© 2021 Poetry Nation Review
All rights reserved
ISBN 978-1-80017-069-8
ISBN 0144-7076

Subscriptions—6 issues
INDIVIDUAL–print and digital:
£39.50; abroad £49
INSTITUTIONS–print only:
£76; abroad £90
INSTITUTIONS–digital only:
from Exact Editions (https://shop.exacteditions.com/gb/pn-review)
to: PN Review, Alliance House, 30 Cross Street, Manchester, M2 7AQ, UK.

Supported by